The Sound

of Sheer Silence
and the
Killing State

Now there was a great wind . . .
but Yahweh was not in the wind;
and after the wind an earthquake,
but Yahweh was not in the earthquake;
and after the earthquake a fire,
but Yahweh was not in the fire;
and after the fire a sound of sheer silence.
—1 Kings 19:12

Studies in Peace and Scripture Series

Volumes in the Studies in Peace and Scripture Series are sponsored by the Institute of Mennonite Studies, Elkhart, Indiana, and released by a variety of publishers.

TheSound
ofSheerSilence
and the
KillingState
THE DEATH PENALTY
AND THE BIBLE

Millard Lind

Foreword by Howard Zehr

Studies in Peace and Scripture Series, Volume 8

Publishing House
the new name of Pandora Press U.S.
Telford, Pennsylvania

copublished with
Herald Press
Scottdale, Pennsylvania

Cascadia Publishing House orders, information, reprint permissions:
contact@CascadiaPublishingHouse.com
1-215-723-9125
126 Klingerman Road, Telford PA 18969
www.CascadiaPublishingHouse.com

The Sound of Sheer Silence and the Killing State
Copyright © 2004 by
Cascadia Publishing House, Telford, PA 18969
All rights reserved
Copublished with Herald Press, Scottdale, PA
Library of Congress Catalog Number: 2004006676
ISBN: 1-931038-23-6
Printed in the United States by G. B. Printing, Logan Township, NJ
Book design by Cascadia Publishing House
Cover design by Jonathan Peachey

The paper used in this publication is recycled and meets the
minimum requirements of American National Standard for Information Sci-
ences—Permanence of Paper for Printed Library Materials, ANSI Z39.48-
1984.1984

Library of Congress Cataloguing-in-Publication Data
Lind, Millard, 1918-
The sound of sheer silence and the killing state : the death penalty
and the Bible / Millard Lind.-- 1st ed.
    p. cm. -- (Studies in peace and scripture series ; v. 8)
Includes bibliographical references.
ISBN 1-931038-23-6 (trade pbk. : alk. paper)
1. Capital punishment--Biblical teaching. 2. Capital punishment--Re-
ligious aspects--Mennonites. I. Title. II. Series: Studies in peace and
scripture ; v. 8.

BS680.C3L56 2004
261.8'3366--dc22

                                                        2004006676

    12 11 10 09 08 07 06 05 04 04   10 9 8 7 6 5 4 3 2 1

*To the community at
Greencroft,
where I wrote this book*

CONTENTS

PART TWO: RETROSPECT AND PROSPECT

Foreword

AFTER A SHORT MORATORIUM, the United States has returned to its historical attachment to death as a penalty for serious wrongdoing. Indeed, executions have become so common place that we hardly notice them. Yet revelations about the sentencing and execution of innocent people have caused reservations among even the strongest proponents—if not about the death penalty itself, at least about the difficulty of administering it fairly and accurately.

The question of capital punishment is indeed one of the most urgent ones of our era. It is important because of the concrete reality and implications of the penalty itself. But the question is also urgent because of the symbolic dimensions of the death penalty. What are we saying when we advocate for it? Are we genuinely committed to death as a penalty, or are we rather expressing other concerns, such as the need for decisive responses to wrongdoing or the level of disorder in our society? What does the death penalty as a symbol communicate to others about the value of life or the acceptability of violence? Does it communicate what we intend, or does it convey the opposite?

The death penalty can and should be explored on many levels. Does it deter potential offenders or brutalize society, possibly encouraging more violence? Are the costs more than we can afford? Does it truly represent just desserts for murder?

A question pertinent to my own work is this one: Is the death penalty satisfying to family and friends of homicide victims? To explore this question a recent conference at Skidmore College brought together a diverse range of abolitionists and death penalty supporters, victims and victim advocates as well as offender advocates. The consensus of this group was that while we can marshal stories on either side, there have been few studies of this important issue.

Working from a restorative justice framework that focuses on victims needs and roles, the emerging field of defense-based victim outreach in death penalty cases does suggest that even survivors who are inclined toward the death penalty often choose to forgo this in favor of having other of their needs and concerns met in the judicial process: needs, for example, for information, involvement, acknowledgment, safety. Still, there is much we do not know about this aspect of the death penalty.

All of these issues are urgent, but the religious dimension is especially significant. This is of course true for Christians who do—or should—base their positions on Scripture and the life of Jesus. But in Western society, this topic is also important for non-Christians. For better or worse, Western culture has been molded in part by understandings of Christian theology; some of us would argue that these understandings are in part distorted, but nevertheless they have been highly influential. As Dutch law professor Herman Bianchi has often said, we need to take a homeopathic approach to this: Like the philosophy of homeopathic medicine, it is going to take a dose of what caused the problem to cure it.

In this book Millard Lind takes on this challenge, but in an unusual way. He identifies key biblical emphases, tracking them through both newer and older Testaments, not shying away from difficult texts, weaving themes together into a whole cloth. Lind has been exploring biblical motifs of justice and injustice, war and peace, for many years. As he suggests in his preface, this book is the culmination of a life of scholarly work, and an alternative to his memoirs. Knowing something about his life journey, I am sure his memoirs would have been interesting. This, however, may be a more significant contribution to one of the most pressing issues of our era.

—*Howard Zehr, Professor of Sociology and Restorative Justice;*
Co-Director, Conflict Transformation Program
Eastern Mennonite University
Harrisonburg, Virginia

Series Preface

V ISIONS OF PEACE ABOUND IN THE BIBLE, whose pages are also filled with the language and the reality of war. In this respect, the Bible is thoroughly at home in the modern world, whether as a literary classic or as a unique sacred text. This is, perhaps, a part of the Bible's realism: bridging the distance between its world and our own is a history filled with visions of peace accompanying the reality of war. That alone would justify study of peace and war in the Bible. However, for those communities in which the Bible is sacred Scripture, the matter is more urgent. For them, it is crucial to understand what the Bible says about peace—and about war. These issues have often divided Christians from each other, and the way Christians have understood them has had terrible consequences for Jews and, indeed, for the world. A series of scholarly investigations cannot hope to resolve these issues, but it can hope, as this one does, to aid our understanding of them.

Over the past century a substantial body of literature has grown up around the topic of the Bible and war. Studies in great abundance have been devoted to historical questions about ancient Israel's conception and conduct of war and about the position of the early church on participation in the Roman Empire and its military. It is not surprising that many of these studies have been motivated by theological and ethical concerns, which may themselves be attributed to the Bible's own seemingly disjunctive preoccupation with peace and, at the same time, with war. If not within the Bible itself, then at least from Aqiba and Tertullian, the question has been raised whether—and if so, then on what basis—those who worship God may legitimately participate in war. With the Reformation, the churches divided on this question. The division was unequal, with the majority of Christendom agreeing that, however regrettable war may be, Christians have biblical warrant for participating in it. A minority countered that, however necessary war may appear, Christians have a biblical mandate to avoid it. Modern historical studies have served to bolster one side of this division or the other.

Meanwhile, it has become clear that a narrow focus on participation in war is not the only way, and likely not the best way, to approach the Bible on the topic of peace. War and peace are not simply two sides of the same coin; each is broader than its contrast with the other. Despite agreement on this point, the number of studies devoted to the Bible and peace is still quite small, especially in English. Consequently, answers to the most basic questions remain to be settled. Among these questions is that of what the Bible means in speaking of *shalom* or *eirene*, the Hebrew and the Greek terms usually translated into English as "peace."

By the same token, what the Bible has to say about peace is not limited to its use of these two terms. Questions remain about the relation of peace, in the Bible, to considerations of justice, integrity, and—in the broadest sense—salvation. And of course there still remains the question of the relation between peace and war. In fact, what the Bible says about peace is often framed in the language of war. The Bible very often uses martial imagery to portray God's own action, whether it be in creation, in judgment against or in defense of Israel, or in the cross and resurrection of Jesus Christ—actions aimed at achieving peace.

This close association of peace and war, to which we have already drawn attention, presents serious problems for the contemporary appropriation of the Bible. Are human freedom, justice, and liberation—and the liberation of creation—furthered or hindered by the martial, frequently royal, and pervasively masculine terms in which the Bible speaks of peace? These questions cannot be answered by the rigorous and critical exegesis of the biblical texts alone; they demand serious moral and theological reflection as well. But that reflection will be substantially aided by exegetical studies of the kind included in this series, even as these studies will be illumined by including just that kind of reflection within them.

While we usually consider war and peace to be matters of international politics, the present volume addresses a subject of domestic policy, and domestic violence: capital punishment. By way of examining biblical and other texts, Professor Millard Lind here shows that capital punishment deserves the same kind of analysis and critique devoted to large-scale use of lethal violence for political ends. His work contributes to and expands the purposes of the series.

"Studies in Peace and Scripture" is sponsored by the Institute of Mennonite Studies, the research agency of the Associated Mennonite Biblical Seminary. The seminary and the tradition it represents have a particular interest in peace and, even more so, an abiding interest in the Bible. We hope that this ecumenical series will contribute to a deeper understanding of both.

—*Ben C. Ollenburger, Old Testament Editor,* and
   Willard M. Swartley, New Testament Editor

Author's Preface

You shall not kill.
—Moses and Jesus: Exodus 20:13; Matt. 19:18 (RSV)

ABOUT TWO YEARS AGO, A FRIEND ASKED ME, "When are you going to write your memoirs?" In lieu of my memoirs, this book is a summation of a lifetime, for which I am indebted to many persons. I grew up in a home and congregation that emphasized peace, including non-participation in America's wars.[1] I was first introduced to a rigorous teaching on biblical pacifism and nonresistance at Goshen College, under the tutelage of such persons as H. S. Bender and Guy F. Hershberger.

My first inductive study of the issue of peace and violence in the Old Testament against the background of Near Eastern culture resulted in my writing the book, *Yahweh Is a Warrior: The Theology of Warfare in the Old Testament.* This work was based on my doctoral dissertation written in a Presbyterian seminary under the guidance of David Noel Freedman, then later refined by many patient students and colleagues in my teaching at Associated Mennonite Biblical Seminary.[2] If one type of pacifism may be defined as the theopolitical establishment of a law community upon Yahweh's redemptive covenant or treaty pact rather than upon a violent military act of the human community, this volume sets forth an underlying pacifist tradition of the Old Testament that begins at Sinai and is matured in the Jesus-Messianic event of the first century A.D.

A second book relating to the subject of the Old Testament and a pacifism of trust and undergirding my present work is

Ben Ollenburger's *Zion, City of the Great King: A Theological Symbol of the Jerusalem Cult*.[3] In this exegetical study of three Zion Psalms (Psalms 46, 48, 76) and of Isaiah's prophetic directives to Judah's Davidic king when war threatened (Isa. 7-8), Ollenburger discovers that Yahweh as Creator promises to defend Zion-Jerusalem. This promise, like the promise to the people at the Sea which formed the basis for the Mosaic covenant, is equally central to the Zion-Davidic covenant (Exod. 14:13-14; Isaiah 7:4, 9b).

A third book important to my present work is that of Christopher D. Marshall's *Beyond Retribution: A New Testament Vision for Justice, Crime, and Punishment*.[4] Ironically, due to my oversight the contents of this volume were unknown to me until after I had nearly completed this work—though the author includes my name in its preface! Marshall's treatise is superior to my own in the area of recent New Testament scholarship, his specialty, especially in Pauline studies, and in its orientation to the general theme of retribution and restorative justice. The two books are significantly different, however, in that they have different intentions and are aimed at a different readership. Hopefully they complement and reinforce each other. I footnoted Marshall's work, though too lightly, after the writing of my manuscript was basically finished.

For time to study Near Eastern law, I am indebted to the encouragement of Marlin Miller, former president of Associated Mennonite Biblical Seminary, and to modest grants of money from Mennonite institutions. At the turn of the millennium, the College Mennonite Church invited me to lead a group in the study of the Sermon on the Mount. This formed the base for the New Testament segment of this book.

I am grateful to many authors, especially to Ulrich Luz, *Matthew 1–7, A Continental Commentary*; Hans Dieter Betz, *The Sermon on the Mount (Hermeneia)*; and Robert Leicht in "2000 Jahre in Widerspruch," a series of eight articles in *Die Zeit* (March 31, to May 20, 1999). For the Introduction that follows this preface, in which I survey the church's attitude toward capital punishment across the centuries, I rely considerably on George MeGivern's book, *The Death Penalty: An Historical and Theological Survey* (2001).

I owe special thanks to my editors, Willard M. Swartley and Ben C. Ollenburger, who accepted this book as a part of their Studies in Peace and Scripture Series and generously gave me of their time. I have warm feelings of gratitude to my publisher, Michael A. King, whose contract for publishing this book lay on my desk for more than a year before I could demonstrate to myself that I still had the energy to write one more book.

I thank also Mary H. Schertz, director of the Institute of Mennonite Studies, who arranged to have the first writing of this manuscript read and critiqued by the AMBS seminary faculty. I am indebted to my family, including Miriam Sieber Lind, who made innumerable suggestions for the manuscript's readability; Matthew who helped me understand my computer; Sarah who corrected my Akkadian; Timothy who saved the project from collapse by taking over as a private journalistic editor/agent; and the other members of my family who, both adoptive and birthed—sons and daughters-in-law, grandchildren, and great-grandchildren—provided an emotional context for this writing.

It is my hope that this book will contribute to an improvement of United States society and in some small way contribute to a precipitous demise of the death penalty in America.

—*Millard C. Lind*
Goshen, Indiana

INTRODUCTION: THE TRIUMPH OF THE CROSS

[God] disarmed the rulers and authorities and made a public example of them, triumphing over them in [the cross].
—Colossians 2:15

CAPITAL PUNISHMENT IN AMERICA

Although every other developed nation in the West has abandoned capital punishment, in America the death penalty is a booming business.[5] The *New York Times Book Review* states that in just a decade "the execution rate has gone up 800 percent," that in 1999 more Americans were executed than in any year since 1952. Over 3500 prisoners now await their destiny on death row, an all-time record.[6]

Austin Sarat, an American professor of jurisprudence and political science, says of capital punishment in America,

> At the turn of the century, capital punishment is alive and well as one of the most prominent manifestations of our killing state, defying the predictions of many scholars who thought it would fade away long ago. Despite the recent reawakening of some abolitionist activity and a modest decline in public support for the death penalty, today more than two-thirds of Americans say they favor capital punishment for persons convicted of murder. Scholars report

23

that vengeance, retribution and the simple justice of an "eye for an eye" sort provide the basis for much of this support.[7]

Today in America, the strongest supporters of "vengeance, retribution and the simple justice of 'an eye for an eye'" include a significant part of the evangelical Christian community. This is documented by programs on television and by occasional interviews on news networks. Nevertheless, the vanguard of present day biblical scholarship, including evangelical scholarship, does not understand biblical justice—as proclaimed by either Testament—primarily as one of "vengeance, retribution, and the simple justice of an 'eye for an eye.' " That concept was challenged over a half-century ago in a paper presented to the ecumenical church by Gerhard von Rad. Von Rad claims that biblical justice is to be understood within the personal structures of covenant.[8] There has been growing scholarly agreement on this point ever since.

Since most evangelicals have a high regard for the Bible, and since many Americans claim a relationship to the church, there should be interest in what the Bible says about law and the death penalty from this perspective of covenant justice.[9]

THE REDEMPTIVE PURPOSE OF SINAI LAW

This book uses the American experience in capital punishment not as a case study, but as a contemporary referent from which to ask the question about state killing in the Bible. Why is the ancient biblical story about the Israelite journey on capital punishment so important for America today? Because over three thousand years ago, on this issue the Israelites were where America is today, at least as far as the law codes are concerned. The ancient Israelites began with a law collection which, though founded on prophetic covenant,[10] includes the penalty of capital punishment. But in the course of a violent history, certain canonical prophets of the ninth and eighth centuries B.C. and perhaps other narrative writers even before that, question capital punishment and move toward a policy of redemption and rehabilitation.

Does biblical religion in the eighth century make a fundamental change from a foundation of retribution and vengeance to one of love and mercy? Hardly! Although this ninth-eighth century prophetic development is a significant breakthrough, as we shall see, this is not merely the result of a general "progressive revelation," moving gradually from an initial position of retribution and vengeance to one of redemption and rehabilitation, thus contradicting Sinai law. Rather, the eighth century change is consistent with the fundamentals of Sinai law, certainly as represented by our present text. It is in part the result of certain tensions caused by the Yahweh covenant within which Sinai law and its death penalty is situated, and which forms that law's constitution.[11]

This tension between constitution and law code, between redemption and retribution, initiated at Sinai over three thousand years ago, challenges the Near Eastern, vengeance-oriented law that continues in America to the present. While giving enough stability to the covenant social order to do its business, the experience at Sinai forever thereafter destabilizes law from the "static," power-oriented law of the Near East. As developed by the prophets, it moves law toward Jesus of Nazareth who, as he claims, universalizes and fulfills it.

In a famous case in which certain Jewish leaders appeal to Jesus, "Now in the law Moses commanded us to stone [execute] such a woman," Jesus stops them in their tracks, reminding them that at the bar of the law, they too deserve death. As they slink off, he says to the woman, "Neither do I condemn you; go your way, and from now on, do not sin again" (John 8:3-11).[12]

In the latter part of this Introduction, I summarize James J. Megivern's account of how the church from post-biblical to modern times nearly lost, then recovered, the achievement of this prophetic journey from Sinai to Jesus. In chapters 1–4, I return to the biblical narrative to trace ancient Israel's trek on this issue: from Moses, to Elijah and the prophets, to Jesus, with a summary in chapter 5. Finally in chapter 6, through a conversation with two law professors as represented in Austin Sarat's book *When the State Kills,* and Thomas L. Shaffer's book, *Moral Memoranda from John Howard Yoder,* I reflect briefly on how the covenant community might resurrect a tension with the American legal system—one based on power politics and violence.

People who live in community have a need for just relationships. If relationships are seriously violated, the resulting dispute is sometimes settled in court, according to law. These laws often develop over many years and are the product of how people have settled disputes in the past. They are usually based on religious or philosophical principles embedded deeply within a society as the society relates itself to divinity and to the universe.

An example of such development of law may be found in Jethro's advice to his son-in-law, Moses.[13] Jethro counsels,

> "You should represent the people before God and you should bring their cases before God [who has delivered you from the Egyptians and from Pharaoh, cf. 18:10]; teach them the statutes and instructions and make known to them the way they are to go and the things they are to do" (Exod. 18:19-20). Then Jethro tells Moses to "look for able men among all the people, men who fear God, are trustworthy, and hate dishonest gain. . . . Let them sit as judges for the people at all times; let them bring every case to you, but decide every minor case themselves." (Exod. 18:19-21)

For our purpose, this Scripture suggests at least three things. First, the appointed judges are to decide "every minor case themselves." These minor decisions are called "case law," legal decisions made mainly by the Israelite "secular courts," presumably at the village gates or within the family clans (cf. Exod. 21:2-11, 21:18-22:17). Such case laws in the present Sinai *covenant code* (Exod. 20:22-23:33) compare most closely with the case law of ancient Near East legal codes (though as individual laws even they often differ significantly in content).

Second, Moses—and his priestly prophetic successors—are to "bring their cases before God (18:19b) [who has delivered you from the Egyptians and from Pharaoh," cf. 18:10]. As we shall see, this further priestly prophetic reorientation of case law within a covenantal worship setting is what gives to Hebrew law much of its peculiar revolutionary character and power.

Third, Moses is to "teach [the people] the statutes and instructions and make known to them the way they are to go and the things they are to do" (Exod. 18:20). This means that besides referring to law to settle an already violated relationship, as these laws had done individually in the village setting, the people need to know what is expected of them beforehand so they can deal justly with their neighbor and avoid disputes. This is likely the main function of the *law summaries* scattered throughout the Bible, and the *law codes* of the Pentateuch—and even of other comparable ancient Near East codes.[14]

The various Near East law codes are first gathered and written down when peoples from different city-states and backgrounds are forced together by conquest to form an empire. To do business, they need to know what justice in the empire demands. Similarly, though the law is that of an intertribal covenant community rather than imperial law, Sinai law is given by Yahweh through the priestly prophetic person, Moses,[15] to the disparate clans so that they know how to be "God's priestly kingdom and holy nation." Instead of uniting the world by dominating it militarily, as do the empires, their mission is to lead the nations in a different way. They are to exemplify a truly just community *by obedience to covenant law* (Exod. 19:4-6; cf. Amos 3:9), from which the nations may then learn to reshape their violent behavior, both for international and domestic relations (cf. Isaiah 2:2-5; Micah 4:1-5).

In the Pentateuch, the first of the canonical legal summaries is the Decalogue (Exod. 20:1-21), while the first of the law codes is the covenant code (Exod. 20:22-23:33).[16] It is primarily this Decalogue and covenant code, with their introduction and conclusion (Exod. 19:3–24:8), that I refer to in this essay—to Moses as he receives them on Mount Sinai, to Elijah as he reassesses them at Sinai-Horeb; and to Jesus as he fulfills them in his Sermon on the (Galilean-Sinai) Mount. On the basis of this discussion, my intent is to make a connection as to how the church and synagogue, with their redemptive covenant law, might influence contemporary state law—state law with its foundation of what is essentially still ancient imperial law based on violent power and retribution.[17]

Moses at Sinai begins this revolution in Near Eastern law and justice. I note first how this Sinai law, like other Near Eastern law, includes the death penalty and *lex talionis* (law of retaliation or "eye for an eye"). Sinai law has major differences, however, which, as the story suggests,[18] arise out of the tension of human case law with Yahweh's theophany and covenant (cf. Exod. 18:19-20, 22). This theophany and covenant provide a new motive and model for law: Yahweh's historic deliverance of Israel from state slavery and infinite forgiveness for those who commit themselves to Yahweh and this divine way of freedom. This *Nachfolge Jahweh* (imitation of Yahweh's saving acts for Israel) ultimately is to be the pattern not only for Israel's foreign relations but also for its domestic relations and for its vocation as a priestly kingdom representing the way of God to the nations (Exod. 19:6; 20:2, 6).

Elijah's pilgrimage to Sinai-Horeb clarifies for him how Yahweh differs from the Baal-like gods of the Near East on this very point. Yahweh is represented on the earthly scene primarily by the persecuted prophet Elijah, rather than by the human offices of Near East kingship; by the "sound of sheer silence" as heard by the prophet rather than by "wind, earthquake and fire"—nature's powers represented on the societal level by kingship and the armed services (1 Kings 19:11-12).

Throughout the books of Kings, this leadership of "the law and the prophets"—with its concept of freedom and forgiveness—struggles on the political plane to overtake the natural human inclination of "law and retribution." Yahweh's triumph over retribution is envisioned especially in the prophetic books, from the eighth century Hosea, Amos and Isaiah to the exilic period of Ezekiel, the Servant Songs of Isaiah 40-55, and to the late apocalyptic book of Daniel (164 B.C.).

This triumph is initiated, however, not by the later prophets, but by early Sinai law, by the motive-model introduction to its Covenant Anticipation, "You have seen what I did to the Egyptians, and how I bore you on eagles' wings and brought you to myself." (Exod. 19:4); and by the two motive-model clauses[19] of the Decalogue that form an inclusion around the commandments that prohibit the worship of other gods and worship of idols: "I am Yahweh your God who brought you out of the land of Egypt, out of the house of slavery" (Exod. 20:2), and "I am Yahweh your God, a jealous God, punishing children for the iniquities of parents, to the third and fourth generations of those who reject me, but showing *stead-*

fast love to the thousandth generation of those who love me and keep my commandments" (Exod. 20:6, emph. added).

This model and motivating reference to the Israelite experience in Egypt is also attached to three individual laws of the covenant code (Exod. 22:21; 23:9, 15). This illustrates how the exodus experience of freedom is to be a model for and to motivate Israel's "secular" law, as these individual cases are brought "before God;" that is, as they are proclaimed by the priest-prophet to the worshiping congregation (Exod. 22:21; 23:9; cf. 18:19). Thus Yahweh's action for Israel becomes a generalized guide for the lawful life of the future.

The good news of Jesus' Sermon on the Mount is that law as covenant love moves decisively from concept to fulfillment in Jesus. This is fulfillment of the intent of Sinai law.[20] This intent is indicated in the Sermon by the principles stated in the petitions of the Lord's Prayer (Matt. 6:9-13), and by the practical commands of the six antitheses (Matt. 5:21-48), reaffirming and expanding the inwardness of the Decalogue.

With the fifth antithesis I will discuss especially Paul's statement on subjection to the governing authorities (Rom. 13:1-7). I will attempt to show that legitimate societal and state law standards are minimal levels of proverb and law, below which society is not to fall. As such, even though they are not eschatologically relevant, they are to be respected and drawn into tension with the forward movement of divine grace as defined by covenant law. This covenant law precedes and follows Paul's statement about the Roman state and is to be the model for the new community to which Paul is writing.

Clarence Bauman says of the relationship between Jesus' Sermon on the Mount and Sinai law,

> The Pentateuchal motifs in Matthew present Jesus in a positive relation to Moses. The parallels in setting and content between the Sermon on the Mount and the Decalogue portray Jesus as the messianic fulfillment of the Mosaic prototype. The 'new Moses' is not opposed to his forerunner and his demands are not antithetical to the commandments from Sinai. This Mosaic typology is meant to confirm the mountain teaching of Jesus from the perspective of Sinai. Mosaic categories are transcended in that the Messianic

> Torah reflects the personal authority of the Lord Messiah
> (Matt. 7:24, 28), whose call to faith is at once an invitation to
> *Nachfolge Christi* [to emulate Christ] and whose instruction
> in righteousness is training in *imitatio Christi* [to imitate
> Christ].[21]

Independently of Bauman, I have come to a similar conclusion: that there is primarily a positive relationship between Sinai law and Jesus' Sermon that should be reflected in honest research. This positive relation is not arbitrarily invented: the Sermon on the Mount fulfills the *intent* of Sinai law as this is stated, for example, by its covenant or constitution (Exod. 19:4-6; 24:1-8; 20:1-6). The case law of Sinai, however, still includes capital punishment (Exod. 21:29), a contradiction which the prophets and Jesus more than overcome.[22]

While the intent of the Sermon is Nachfolge Christi, to emulate God in Christ, the intent of Sinai law is Nachfolge Jahweh: that in its own interhuman relationships, Israel is to emulate God's action of saving Israel from state slavery (Exod. 19:4; 20:2; 22:21-22; 23:9). I intend to show how God's saving action for Israel (and through Israel for the nations) severely limits and then rejects the principle of retribution of Near East kingship law (Exod. 20:5). It extends to infinity the principles of mercy and forgiveness of those who love God and who are committed to keep the divine commandment (Exod. 20:6). This freedom-giving God and the qualified "opposite-sidedness" of the divine character—severe restriction of retribution, and forgiveness to infinity—Israel is to emulate, not only in its domestic relations, but ultimately in its foreign relations as stated, for example, in the prophetic book of Jonah.[23] Finally, God establishes the new universal order "in Christ." To herald this, the gospel writers place the entire Jesus narrative of words and deeds under his passion and resurrection.

THE BIBLICAL CASE
AGAINST CAPITAL PUNISHMENT

There are of course utilitarian reasons that weigh against capital punishment, such as the observation that it does not deter crime, that it cannot be justly implemented, and that it is expensive. Although such reasons are important and deserve discussion, they are not the subject of this book.[24] And such reasons become idolatrous if they supplant the central religious concept of justice and its personal concern, a concern directed toward both the individual and the corporate body, as we shall see. It is mainly this personal concern—basic to covenant justice and law, Yahweh's saving action and steadfast love for Israel and for the world, to be emulated on the societal level—that I propose to trace from Moses to Elijah to Jesus. I oppose capital punishment because from the perspective of the God revealed in the Bible, determined in my view from a careful reading of the text as attempted below, capital punishment is *wrong*. In this book, the ancient Israelite and modern American problem of capital punishment and its answer are used as an example of the unity of biblical ethics with theology, that both ethics and theology are rooted in the Israelite experience with God, and are of prime importance to our twenty-first century problem, which is the killing state.

This book is a summation of a lifetime of teaching and writing. It concludes that Sinai law is a center, perhaps *the* center of the Bible's social-theological proclamation.[25] If this conclusion is correct, then covenant law, which is more than the sum of its two component parts, covenant *and* law, is the epitome of the biblical adage: "The stone which the builders rejected, has become the head of the corner" (Ps. 118:22; Matt. 21:42). And the Bible is again unveiled as a new, vital unity.

I do not pretend to pursue this conclusion in all its biblical ramifications. Rather, I attempt inductively to sketch out the claim of Sinai law's centrality and its development in the Bible. I work throughout primarily with the biblical text. But the Bible itself claims as its context the cultures of the ancient Near East and Mediterranean Basin, and today's students of Sinai law place it within the context of an extensive legal literature, much of which has been dug up from the sands of the Near East by archaeologists in the last century and a half. For comparative purposes I limit myself mainly to the eighteenth-century B. C. Hammurabi law code that was distributed widely in time and space throughout the ancient Near East. However, I have read much more widely than that law, and consider this much larger fund of literature for my results.

INTERPRETING THE BIBLE

Within the Bible itself, my method of interpretation is wholistic; that is, I interpret the details of the present text within the context of the main themes of each biblical book.[26] Though I acknowledge the importance of historical and form critical exegesis in which I have been trained, these must contribute to an understanding of the present canonical text. While I attempt here to speak to the American public, I include notes to clearly indicate the dependence and relation of my thought to the international community of biblical and Near East scholarship, and to suggest additional resources for the more serious reader.

A wholistic method includes for me an emphasis on the unity of the Bible, including the unity of the Old and New Testaments. This is not to disparage the study of the Bible's disunities, many reflecting the yaw and backpedaling of Israelite history from the forward thrust of covenant law. (For a sketch of a similar backpedaling in the Christian story, see below, *The Church And Capital Punishment: From Second Century Polemicists To The Postmodern Era*.) These parts are to be interpreted and sometimes critiqued in terms of the overarching themes of the various biblical books and of the Bible's overarching trajectories.[27] By identifying empathetically with the faith of the biblical writers, an attempt is made, however imperfectly, to note some key hermeneutical critiques within the biblical story itself.[28] The study of the parts, while important, should not become a diversion from the Bible's major themes.

Contemporary biblical studies presently result in the lessening of the historic polarization of church and synagogue on the central theme of law.[29] Though sometimes the synagogue, like the church, has fallen into legalism, throughout the centuries it has assumed law to be within the relational context of covenant. And frontline Christian scholarship is presently questioning its past interpretation of the apostle Paul's presumed negative attitude to law.[30] While we are indeed saved by grace alone, our salvation will be judged by our works, our obedience from the heart to covenant law.[31] For those who accept these corrections, covenant law and its development presents a unified, positive theme throughout the Bible, a trajectory beginning with Sinai and extending to the Sermon of Jesus, as stated by his gospel and epistolary interpreters.

The Protestant church's historically negative attitude toward biblical law runs parallel with many Christian's acceptance of the sovereignty of state law. This acceptance of state sovereignty may contribute to America's unleashed capitalism with its attendant evils of social stratification, oppression, and imperialistic wars. Or, it may justify state killing, especially of the weak and poor.[32] In more dysfunctional states, it has been used to legitimate the holocaust and ethnic cleansing. "Free from the law" has not necessarily produced an "O happy condition"[33]

THE CHURCH AND CAPITAL PUNISHMENT: FROM SECOND-CENTURY POLEMICISTS TO THE POSTMODERN ERA

Felix Manz, the first Anabaptist martyr, is executed in Switzerland in 1527 A.D. One of his several indictments is that he challenges the states' right to inflict capital punishment.[34] In 1556—still two centuries before the Enlightenment—Menno Simons, a Holland Anabaptist who lives under threat of execution for most of his ministry, writes to Martin Micron about the death penalty,

> I said nothing more to you than that it would hardly become a true Christian ruler to shed blood. For this reason, If the transgressor should truly repent before his God and be reborn of Him, he would then also be a chosen sainted and child of God, a fellow partaker of grace, a spiritual member of the Lord's body, sprinkled with His precious blood and anointed with His Holy Ghost, a living grain of the Bread of Christ and an heir to eternal life; and for such an one to be hanged on the gallows, put on the wheel, placed on the stake, or in any manner be hurt in body or goods by another Christian, who is of one heart, spirit, and soul with him, would look somewhat strange and unbecoming in the light of the compassionate, merciful, kind nature, disposition, spirit, and example of Christ, the meek Lamb—which example He has commanded all His chosen children to follow.

> Again, if he remain impenitent, and his life be taken,
> one would unmercifully rob him of the time of repentance
> of which, in case his life were spared, he might yet avail
> himself.... [35]

James J. Megivern notes in *The Death Penalty: An Historical and Theological Survey* (1997) that these early modern "heretics" are not alone in Western history to oppose the death penalty. Sketching the responses of the church from biblical times to the present, he reports that the early church fathers who write on the subject, though not in agreement on the state's right to take human life, strongly oppose Christian involvement in such state activities, whether capital punishment or war (100-300 A.D.).[36] Megivern points out that in this period Christians, as members of an illegal religion, were likely targets of the death penalty and may have spoken against it, but as a minority group they would have found it difficult to preserve their protest.

Megivern says that a change in church attitudes toward killing occurs after the emperor Constantine in the fourth century, a change that culminates much later in the Crusades against the Moslems and wars against the "heretics." He reports that a decisive turn in church teaching is made by the medieval theologian, Thomas Aquinas, in the twelfth century A.D. Retribution rather than forgiveness and rehabilitation becomes central in Christian thought on crime and punishment.[37]

But, says Megivern, earlier Christian thought on this subject is recovered by the so-called "heretics" of early modern times whose influence or communal life often continues to this day—the Waldensians (1170s), Wycliffites (mid-fourteenth century), Anabaptists (sixteenth century), Quakers (seventeenth century), and others.[38] Furthermore, Megivern claims that the secular thinkers of the Enlightenment are not original in their important religious and secular contribution against capital punishment but are stimulated in their thought by the early church fathers via these "heretics."[39]

In the present Catholic Church, the turnaround on capital punishment begins with Pope John XXIII and the second Vatican Council (1962-65 AD).[40] The Catholic bishops, he says, are now united consistently against abortion, capital punishment, and war. Today we celebrate that Catholic, Quaker, Mennonite, various Anabaptist-related groups, and other churches and peoples of faith cooperate in opposition to the death penalty, at a time when America's death row grows longer and when such a witness is not politically popular.

Megivern credits Jesus with the united stand against the death penalty on the part of church leaders of the second and third centuries A.D. Jesus himself is executed by crucifixion at the order of a Roman court, a decision the church claims to be made by those outside the covenant law. This decision, they claim, God reverses by resurrection, a reversal which becomes a part of the church's kerygma or preaching: "that God has made him both Lord and Christ, this Jesus whom you crucified" (Acts 2:22-24, 36). One would think that capital punishment might be opposed by the church because in its kerygma it is seen as an act contrary to that of God, an act for which women and men are called to repentance.

As we shall see, concern for the death penalty is characteristic of the community of faith long before Jesus; covenant law from the time of Moses prescribes this penalty for certain infringements, ranging from heresy to adultery, to murder. At the time of the exile, say the prophets, the entire community of Israel suffers death. Speaking figuratively, Ezekiel says that only by resurrection and the gift of a new heart and spirit can Israel be gathered and begin again (Ezek. 36:16-37:14).

Much later, the apostle Paul extends this assessment of deserving to die to everyone, both Gentile and Jew (Rom. 1:18–3:31; esp. 3:23) and therefore says, "in passing judgment on another you condemn yourself. . ." (2:1). The story of the woman caught in the act of adultery who was brought to Jesus by the scribes and Pharisees, is congruent with such traditions: "Now in the law Moses commanded us to stone such women. Now what do you say?" Jesus does not answer her accusers by challenging the integrity of covenant law, but by exposing her accusers—that no one is innocent enough to enforce it: "Let anyone among you who is without sin be the first to throw a stone at her [execute her]." When her accusers slink away, he says, "Neither do I condemn you. Go your way, and from now on do not sin again" (John 8:1-11).

While salvation from slavery in Egypt is interpreted by the apostles as a part of Israel's life-giving story reaching forward toward Jesus, the death penalty is incongruous with that story; it reaches backward toward Hammurabi and the empires of the ancient Near East. Moses and Elijah, associated in the Old Testament with Sinai-Horeb, appear with a transfigured Jesus "on a high mountain" to talk about his imminent death (Matt. 17:1-20; Luke 9:28-36). This death becomes a life-giving event for all who have violated the intention of the law (Rom. 5:6-8). From its beginnings at Sinai, a communal foundation is laid by this gift of covenant law, to give life and rehabilitation to the offender, and in covenant to reconcile victim and offender to God and to one another.

The first three chapters will examine three events in this development of law, events associated with Moses, the prophet Elijah, and Jesus in their respective meetings on the law-mountain (Exod. 19–24; 1 Kings 19; Matt. 5–7).

PART ONE

A SERIES OF THREE: MOSES, ELIJAH, JESUS

And [Jesus] was transfigured before them,
and his face shone like the sun,
and his clothes became dazzling white.
Suddenly there appeared to them Moses
and Elijah talking with him.
—Matthew 17:2-3.

1

On the Mountain with Moses, Exodus 19–24: From Law Based on Retribution to Law Based on Covenant Love

"I am the Yahweh your God who brought you out of the land of Egypt, out of the house of slavery."
—Exodus 20:2

"Yahweh, Yahweh, a God merciful and gracious, slow to anger, and abounding in steadfast love and faithfulness, keeping steadfast love for the thousandth generation, forgiving iniquity and transgression and sin, yet by no means clearing the guilty, but visiting the iniquity of the parents upon children and the children's children to the third and the fourth generation,"
—Exodus 34:6-7; cf. 20:5-6

NEAR EASTERN LAW CODES

At the beginning of the twentieth century. the finding of the Hammurabi law code stimulated a reappraisal of Sinai law[41] and of biblical law as a whole.[42] The discovery of this and many other law collections dug out of the ancient sands of the Near East[43] has pushed the history of Western law back nearly two millennia—from Greek-Roman times in the Mediterranean basin to the times of ancient Sumer in the lower Tigris-Euphrates valley.[44] It took many years for students of ancient Near East cultures to translate and collate that law. It has taken even longer for Bible students to understand Sinai law within that ancient legal context.[45]

To simplify the task of comparing significant similarities and differences of Hebrew law with other Near Eastern codes, I will limit this chapter to the first segment of Sinai law in the Bible, a segment made up of four parts:

(1) an introductory oracle and theophany that anticipates covenant (Exod. 19; esp. vv. 3-6);

(2) the Decalogue and its aftermath that sets forth the general principles of the covenant (20:1-21);

(3) the Covenant Law Code and promise that details individual laws of the covenant (20:22-23:33); and

(4) a conclusion of covenant-making (24:1-8).[46]

To simplify the comparative task from the side of the Near East law codes outside of ancient Israel, I will illustrate common characteristics and differences of these "codes" between biblical law and the text of the Hammurabi law code.[47] The presence of this code throughout the Near East from the seventeenth to the sixth centuries B.C. suggests its classic importance in influencing Near Eastern law.[48] By projecting covenant law against this Near East legal background, the revolutionary character of covenant law will become apparent. As we shall see, its likenesses and differences highlight certain intolerable tensions in covenant law, which in the course of Israel's history, are moved toward resolution.

SIMILARITIES OF THE
SINAI CODE TO THE HAMMURABI CODE

Like other Near East law collections, Sinai law deals with the mundane matters of communal life—property rights (Exod. 20:15; 21:35–22:14), human life issues (Exod. 20:13), family concerns (Exod. 20:12, 17); laws concerning justice (Exod. 20:16), and respect for authority (Exod. 20:12; 22:28).[49] Both Sinai and Hammurabi law include the death penalty[50] and the lex talionis. Here are examples of the death penalty:

1. Sinai Covenant Code:[51]

- "Whoever strikes a person mortally shall be put to death" (Exod. 21:12).
- "Whoever kidnaps a person . . . shall be put to death" (Exod. 21:16).
- "Whoever curses father or mother shall be put to death" (Exod. 21:17).

2. Hammurabi Code:[52]

- "If a seignior [a member of a higher class] has helped either a male slave of the state or a female slave of the state or a male slave of a private citizen or a female slave of a private citizen to escape through the city-gate, he shall be put to death" (Hammurabi #15).
- "If a seignior stole the property of church or state, that seignior shall be put to death; also the one who received the stolen goods from his hand shall be put to death" (Hammurabi #6).
- "If a seignior accused a[nother] seignior and brought a charge of murder against him, but has not proved it, his accuser shall be put to death" (Hammurabi #1).

In this first segment of the Sinai covenant law, the range of crimes that may result in the death penalty are: premeditated murder (Exod. 21:12-13), striking father or mother (21:15), kidnapping (21:16), an owner's liability for a death by an ox known to gore (21:28-32), killing a thief caught in plain daylight (22:2), for being a female sorcerer (22:18), sexual intercourse with an animal (22:19), sacrificing to a god other than Yahweh (22:20)—a total of eight capital cases. These statements of the human death penalty (and the lex talionis) in this first segment of the Sinai pericope are all found within the Covenant Law Code (Exod. 20:22–23:19).

While earlier law codes of Ur-Nammu and Eshnunna have relatively few laws that are capital cases,[53] the Code of Hammurabi makes a giant leap; it has a total of twenty-five such laws. This is in addition to cases of unusual punishment, such as dragging an offender through a field with oxen.[54] This coarsening may be caused by the extent and diversity of Hammurabi's empire, forcing together many peoples who then are no longer bound by local traditions; draconian punishments are prescribed in an attempt to control behavior.

In the Hammurabi Code, the only capital punishment prescribed for murder is for a woman who brings about "the death of her husband because of another man."[55] However, already from around 1900 B.C. murder trials are recovered that prescribe the death penalty for murder.[56] On the other hand, the death penalty in ancient Hittite laws overall has limited use. This is a fact that may suggest possibilities for the contemporary state.

The lex talionis—Latin for "law of retaliation"—is also a common characteristic of Near East law codes, including covenant law. But it is not found in the pre-Hammurabi codes such as those of Lipit-Ishtar and Ur-Nammu. Also, a record of a trial has been recovered from ancient Ugarit (thirteenth century B.C.), which gives compensation as settlement for an inter-city-state case of homicide:

> Before Ini-Teshup, king of Carkemish, Arishimiga, a merchant in the service of the king of Tarhudashshi, and the citizens of Ugarit met in trial. Arishimiga deposed thus: "The citizens of Ugarit killed a merchant of the king of Tarhudashsha." And Arishimiga had not retrieved any of the goods belonging to the merchant who was slain in Ugarit. The king then decided their case thus: "Let Arishimiga take the oath (in support of his testimony) and the citizens of Ugarit shall then pay the full compensation for that merchant." Arishimiga then took the oath, and the citizens of Ugarit paid the full compensation of 180 shekels of silver to Arishimiga, servant of the king of Tarhudashshi. In future time, Arishimiga shall enter no (further) claim against the citizens of Ugarit in respect of the merchant who was slain, and the citizens of Ugarit shall enter no claim against Arishimiga in respect of the 180 shekels of silver of their compensation payment. Whichever (of them) does so enter a claim—this document will prevail against him.[57]

Also, in a letter from a Hittite king to the king of Babylon in about 1270 B.C., that king explains that "the slaying of Babylonian merchants in N Syria could only be redressed through compensation, and that it was not customary for the Hittites to give the death penalty for murder. . . . "[58] Compensation was practiced instead of the lex talionis among the Hittites.

Richard Hasse lists seventeen lex talionis laws in Hammurabi's code.[59] A few examples of these laws are that—

- "If a man has destroyed the sight of another similar person, they shall destroy his sight."[60]
- "If a man has destroyed the eye of a man's son they shall destroy his sight."[61]
- "If a man has knocked out the tooth of a man who is his colleague, they shall knock out his tooth"[62]

If one compares this number with one occurrence of the formula in each of the Covenant, Holiness and Deuteronomy Codes, one can hardly say that the lex talionis formula is *the* characteristic of biblical law. In Exodus 21:23 the full formula appears in connection with a miscarriage occasioned by a pregnant woman who is injured amid a brawl:

> When people who are fighting injure a pregnant woman so that there is a miscarriage, and yet no further harm follows, the one responsible shall be fined what the woman's husband demands, paying as much as the judges determine. If any harm follows, then you shall give life for life, eye for eye, tooth for tooth, hand for hand, foot for foot, burn for burn, wound for wound, stripe for stripe[63] (cf. Lev. 24:19-20; Deut. 19:15-21).

Precisely what happens to the woman, and perhaps to the fetus, is to be done to the perpetrator. But it is not likely that the formula was understood literally in ancient Israel of pre-exile times. We have already noted that in law codes before Hammurabi, money sums were stipulated for injuries to body parts,[64] which compares with modern insurance practice. Immediately after the statement of the lex talionis in Exodus 21, another "equivalent" replaces it, freedom for the slave (21:26-27). The point of the formula both here and throughout the Near East is not likely revenge but punishment that does not exceed the crime—limitation of retribution.[65]

The outstanding biblical narrative to include a formula approximating that of the lex talionis is that of God's blessing of Noah and his sons after the flood. (Gen. 9:6), ushering in a new age in which not humanity, but God is changed (Gen. 9:1).[66] As in the creation story, God gives humanity dominion over *everything*, but now, in addition to plants, permits people to eat animals as food (cf. Gen.1:28-29).

There are, however, two restrictions to this dominion. First, humans are to recognize the sacredness of all of life by not eating animal "flesh with its life," its blood (cf. Lev. 17:10-14). This principle was later accepted at the Jerusalem conference, to be observed by Christian Gentiles (Acts 15:29) and was later taken over by Islam. It recognizes that God is concerned for animals (cf. Jonah 4:11; Matt. 6:26-29). After the flood, the covenant of peace is made not only with human beings, but also with "every living creature" (Gen. 9:12).

This first restriction, respect for animal life, is closely related to the second—prohibition against murder. Brutality toward animals and murder of humans are here connected.[67] On this second restriction God says, "And from human beings, each one for the blood of another, I will require a reckoning for human life" (Gen. 9:5). Then follows the statement,

Whoever sheds the blood of a human,
 by a human shall that person's blood be shed;
 for in his own image God made humankind. (Gen. 9:6)

Eugene Roop says of this poem, "Despite its history of interpretation, Genesis 9:6 does not authorize and promote capital punishment."[68] Those who regard this statement as demanding capital punishment, see it as a judicial formula, a law. Claus Westermann says of this, "The embarrassment remains that the interpreters vary between judicial formula, proverb, and prophetic admonition."[69] The argument that it is a proverb is based on its structure, which is parallel to the statement of Jesus: "All who take the sword will perish by the sword" (Matt. 26:52). But whether command or proverb, it is set within a context that demands a reckoning (9:5); it is a serious violation.

The warning of this "proverb" or threat of "law" is precisely what Cain fears after he kills Abel (Gen. 4:14). Then God places a mark on him to protect this first murderer from the retribution he fears. This act presages other acts and discussions that follow, such as Yahweh's commitment in response to Abraham's appeal for justice in regard to the destruction of Sodom:

"If I find at Sodom fifty righteous in the city, I will forgive the whole place for their sake"—then for the sake of "forty-five," then "forty," then "thirty," then "twenty," and finally, "ten" (Gen. 18: 26-32). Such commitments by Yahweh to forgive the wickedness of an entire city because of the righteousness of a few draw into tension such "laws" or "proverbs" as Genesis 9:6, suggesting different possibilities.[70] This leads to a discussion of essential differences between Hebrew and Near East law.

THE RADICAL REVOLUTION OF COVENANT LAW

Because of these similarities—which at the turn of the twentieth century shocked the Western Christian community—it has taken some time to note significant differences of Sinai law from other Near Eastern law, and the implications of these differences for future Western law.[71] For our purposes I will discuss four major differences of the Sinai law. These differences, obviously interdependent and overlapping, are: the prophetic covenant structure of Sinai law; its model-motive clause; its inclusion of laws regulating both divine-human and interhuman relationships, and finally, the egalitarian nature of Sinai law. I will discuss these differences within the four divisions of this Sinai pericope: The Covenant introduction, the Decalogue, the Covenant Law Code, the Covenant conclusion.

The first major difference between Sinai and other Near Eastern law is most evident in the literary structure of this segment of the Sinai pericope.[72] It is marked off by an inclusio,[73] beginning with Yahweh's oracle *anticipating covenant* (Exod. 19:3-8)[74] and ending with *the consummation of covenant* through the prophetic mediator, Moses[75] (Exod. 24:3-8). After discussing this inclusio, I will compare it with the Prologue and Epilogue of the Hammurabi law code.

> Then Moses went up to God; Yahweh called to him from the mountain, saying, "Thus you shall say to the house of Jacob and tell the Israelites: You have seen what I have done to the Egyptians, and how I bore you on eagles' wings and brought you to myself. Now therefore, if you obey my voice and keep my covenant,[76] you shall be my treasured possession out of all the peoples. Indeed, the whole earth is mine, but you shall be for me a priestly kingdom and a holy

nation. These are the words that you shall speak to the Israelites."[77] (Exod. 19:3:6)

The key word in this inclusio is *covenant* (*berit*, 19:5; 24:7-8);
it occurs in the Pentateuch some twenty times for the Sinai
covenant or its equivalent.[78] Though there are different types of
covenants in the Bible, the term in this context signifies the
legally committed, sworn relationship made between God and
Israel at Sinai , in which Yahweh becomes Israel's God, and Israel becomes Yahweh's people (cf. Josh. 24:16-27; Hosea 2:23;
Heb. 2:25). Covenant is a metaphor adapted from the social
and political arena of the ancient Near East, where covenants
were used to unite unrelated families, clans, tribes, city states,
or empires. The Sinai covenant is a religious-political union
made between God and the disparate clans of the Israelites (vv.
3, 6b), to lead the world in Yahweh's justice.[79] The importance
of covenant for biblical faith is suggested by the titles of the two
divisions of the Christian Bible: the Old and New Covenants
("Testaments").[80]

Strikingly, this covenant inclusio is what may be called a
"prophetic covenant." That is, for the acceptance and enforce-
ment of the law that it envelops, the prophetic figure, Moses
calls the Israelites by Yahweh's oracle to decide for obedience
to covenant law in response to what they have seen that Yahweh has done for them (Exod. 19:4; cf. Josh. 24:14-15). Moses
appeals to their inner motivation by invoking God's act of
grace:[81] Yahweh, rather than Israel's armed services, delivers
them from the oppression of empire and reminds them, "I . . .
brought you to myself," i.e., to this covenant making ceremony
at Sinai.[82] In Yahweh's covenant with Israel, both international
deliverance and covenant law are closely associated acts of
God's grace.[83]

After reminding them of past favors—pacifying Israel's
enemy and bringing Israel to the divine self—Yahweh makes a
promise contingent on Israel's obedience and keeping
covenant. That promise focuses on their vocation: Since the
whole earth belongs to Yahweh, they will be God's "priestly
kingdom," God's "holy nation." That is, by obedience to divine
law ("my voice")—the poetic equivalent of "keeping my
covenant"[84]—they will form a priestly community set apart to

God to lead the nations by the example of their just domestic relationships (cf. Isaiah 2:2-5).[85]

And just as there is no violent power mechanism apparent within this statement of Sinai covenant to enforce Israel's obedience to law, neither is there a human power mechanism provided to achieve its promised vocation in relation to the nations. Both power transformations—for enforcing domestic obedience to law and for implementing its international leadership of the nations—are replaced by Israel's worshipful response to God's grace: *trust in the God who protects from oppressive empires (19:4a)*[86] *and obedience to the God who leads Israel to the divine self to establish covenant law* (19:4b). In both cases, violent coercion is essentially replaced with personal commitment and community with God and fellow worshipers.[87] Israel's vocational calling at Sinai strikes at the heart of the human problem of violence.

This internalizing of law in the *Covenant Anticipation* (Exod. 19:3-6) is concluded in the second half of the inclusio or *Covenant Consummation* (24:3-8). As covenant mediator, Moses does not consummate covenant by setting up structures for response to violence but tells "the people all the words of Yahweh and all the ordinances," to which "all the people" answer: "All the words that Yahweh has spoken we will do" (24:3; cf. v.7). The covenant is sealed with two symbolic acts, the covenant sacrificial meal and the covenant blood ceremony.[88] "Offerings of well-being" *(selamin, 24:6; v.5 in Heb.)* are a shared meal between Yahweh and the offerer, including friends, a meal that seals the pact of unity (cf. Gen. 26:28-30). Yahweh and Israel make up one family; the meal means that they share one life.[89]

The meal is followed by the ritual of blood, which in ancient Israel represents life (cf. Lev. 17:11). Moses dashes half of the basin of blood against the altar, representing Yahweh, and half upon the people (Exod. 24:6, 8), symbolizing again the community of life between God and Israel. This symbolic act is referred to by Jesus in Paul's account of the Lord 's Supper: "This cup is the new covenant in my blood" (1 Cor. 11:25; cf. Matt. 26:28; Mark 14:24; Luke 22:20). In the New Testament, the Sinai covenant is thus identified with this central symbolic act of the church.

HOW THE COVENANT INCLUSIO (EXOD. 19:3-6; 24:3-8) CONTRASTS WITH THE PROLOGUE AND THE EPILOGUE OF THE HAMMURABI CODE

This covenant inclusio, which surrounds and provides a context for understanding Sinai law, may be compared in literary structure with the prologue and epilogue that surrounds and provides a context for understanding the Hammurabi law code.[90] Beyond this literary structure—that is, from the sociological and political point of view—each may be thought of as the constitution or fundamental law of their respective societies by which their law code is shaped and interpreted.[91]

Moving from formal to more substantial matters of the constitution, the two law codes are essentially different. While the introduction and conclusion to Sinai law is a prophetic covenant, the prologue and epilogue of the Hammurabi stelae sets forth mythologically the ancient concept of law within a kingship or power covenant.

> "When lofty Anum[92] . . . (and) Enlil[93] . . . determined for Marduk[94] . . . the Enlil functions over all mankind,[95] . . . called Babylon by its exalted name, made it supreme in the world, established for him in its midst an enduring kingship, whose foundations are as enduring as heaven and earth—at that time Anum and Enlil named me, Hammurabi, the devout and god-fearing prince, to cause justice to prevail in the land, to destroy the wicked and the evil, that the strong might not oppress the weak, to rise like the sun[96] over the black-headed [people],[97] and to light up the land."[98]

With the rise of the Babylonian empire, this political myth proclaims that the sky-god Anum and the storm-god Enlil, respectively leader and chief executive of the Mesopotamian pantheon, appoint Marduk, god of the city, Babylon, to perform Enlil's coercive executive functions "over all mankind." Marduk's appointment means that on the earthly scene Babylon is militarily supreme in the world.

Anum and Enlil, the two chief gods of the pantheon, then appoint Hammurabi to promote the people's "welfare"[99] and to make "justice to prevail in the land." The concept of justice is a worthy one: to provide "good government,"[100] including the protection of the "weak" against oppression; the "orphan" and "widow" are specifically mentioned.[101]

According to this power myth, as "shepherd" king, Hammurabi is in charge of economics; he is to make "affluence and plenty abound"[102] Also, as "devout patron" he is to care for the Mesopotamian temples.[103] Finally, Hammurabi heads up the armed services: He is "the king who has made the four quarters of the world subservient." [104]

As king, Hammurabi mythologically heads up the Babylonian power structure, uniting in himself the powers of law, justice, economics, religion, and the armed services. He is "king of justice;"[105] his law is based on retribution as threatened by the king and his military and police power. Sinai law, on the other hand, is made not between God and king but between God and people, within the structure of prophetic covenant proclaimed by Yahweh and mediated through a prophetic figure, Moses (Exod. 19:3-6; 24:1-8; cf. Hosea 12:13).[106]

Samuel Greengus states that ancient Near Eastern laws are "upheld by the king as part of his duty of government."[107] In contrast, he says of biblical law:

The ultimate authority of laws was seen as coming from God. Here Israelite society was very different from other ANE societies."[108] One difference, Greengus says, has to do with law and ethics: "The linking of God to law added an important ethical dimension to the worldview of ancient Israel. Since God was the source of law, the failure to observe the law became an offense against the deity. This linking . . . also succeeded in placing ethics in the matrix of human history and fostered the concept to which God was also responsibly connected.[109]

Greengus acknowledges that "Covenant is central to the presentation of the Pentateuchal laws and commandments." Although he holds that "The biblical covenants were modeled after the formal agreements or treaties that existed between monarchs and their vassals in the political sphere of the ancient world," he further states that "the concept of a connection between divine covenant and divine law is solely a product of Israelite theology.[110]

As we shall see in chapter 2, this contrast between the constitution of Sinai Covenant Law and that of the Law of Hammurabi on the issue of power politics portrays the major tension not only between Israel and the ancient Near East, but also that which developed within Israel itself, a tension institutionalized within Judah by the covenant between Yahweh and the Davidic dynasty.[111] The most important point of this compromise with Near Eastern law is that the king, with his people, is still to be under authority of Sinai covenant law, including the laws of Yahweh war (cf. Deut. 17: 14-20; 20; Psalms 72; 89).[112]

THE DECALOGUE, EXODUS 20:2-17

Whatever may have been the purpose of the Decalogue in its original life situation, in its present literary context it "delineates the principal obligations of the *holy nation*"[113] (Exod. 19:6, emph. added). As an independent literary form, the Decalogue has a central place in the biblical tradition.[114] It appears twice in the Pentateuch (Exod. 20:1-17; Deut. 5:6-27). It is the only law given directly from Yahweh to the people, unmediated by Moses (Exod. 20:1). The Decalogue is also set apart from other biblical law by being inscribed on two tables of stone (Exod. 31:18; 34:1,28), by a distinctive name (Exod. 34:28), and by deposit into the ark (Exod. 25:16; Deut. 10:1-5). Its commands are reflected in the prophets (Hos. 4:1; Jer. 7:9) and in the Psalms (Psa. 15); and it provides "a framework for the revision of law found in Deuteronomy 12–26."[115]

Later synagogue and church traditions continue to give to the Decalogue this central place. In the later Jewish tradition, the Ten Words are found at Qumran, the Nash papyrus and tefillin,[116] and "some Jewish sources have classified the 613 commandments under the ten headings of the precepts of the Decalogue."[117] In the church, the New Testament highlights some of its commandments in Jesus' antithesis of the Sermon on the Mount (Matt. 5:21-37); the call of the young ruler (Matt. 19:16-30), and in the epistles (Rom. 8:7-13; 13;8-10; Eph. 6:1-4; James 2:8-13). It continues this central place in later Roman Catholic, Lutheran, and Reformed traditions, each one enumerating the commandments somewhat differently. Since Medieval times, Catholic scholars have interpreted it as "a summary of natural law;" while in modern times others have seen it as a declaration of human rights.[118]

As a boy, I learned the typical Sunday school version of the "Ten Commandments," beginning with "Thou shalt." This abbreviated reading, stripping the commandments of their covenantal character, was affirmed by scholarly historical-critical and form-critical revisions of the text.[119] In contrast, a simple literary reading of the present text affirms the covenant relatedness of these commandments: "I am . . . ; you shall" (Exod. 20:2-3). The English term, *Decalogue,* is a transliteration from the Greek version of their Hebrew name, *The Ten Words,* which are identified as the covenant of God with Israel (*'asseret hadebarim,* Exod. 34:28; Deut. 4:13; cf. Deut. 5:2) . The synagogue enumeration of the Decalogue begins with this first Word (Exod. 20:2), which is the foundation for the nine Words that follow.[120]

This first Word is a motive-model sentence[121] that identifies Yahweh as the freedom-giving God who alone is to be worshiped (Exod. 20:2-3; cf. 19:4). It forms an inclusio with a second motive clause marking the boundaries of this first segment of the Decalogue—the sentence and clause each beginning in Hebrew with three identical words: "I am Yahweh your God" (20:2, 5-6, *'anoki YHWH eloheka*). This inclusio envelops three prohibitions, making up the first and second commandment:

I am Yahweh your God who brought you out of the land of Egypt, out of the house of slavery;

[1] you shall have no other gods before me.

[2] You shall not make for yourself an idol. . . .

[3] You shall not bow down to them or worship them;

for I am Yahweh your God, a jealous God, punishing children for the iniquity of parents, to the third and the fourth generation of those who reject me, but showing steadfast love to the thousandth generation of those who love me and keep my commandments (emph. added).[122]

The three negatives—no other gods,[123] no idols,[124] and no worship of either—are prohibitions calling forth Israel's allegiance to Yahweh in gratitude for divine grace: the grace of God's redemption (20:2) and steadfast love (20:5-6), a love placed in an asymmetrical relationship to Yahweh's retribution. For this concluding inclusio radically limits Yahweh's retribution to the extant human family—made up in ancient times of three or four generations— eclipsing this limited retribution with God's "steadfast love" that is to infinity, the "thousandth generation" (cf. Deut. 7:9).[125] A divine logic is at work here.

This inclusio then is not to be regarded as a mere formal "introduction" and "conclusion" to this first segment of the Decalogue. Rather, it is an expression of the essential character of covenant law itself: the model and motivation for that human behavior whose central character is allegiance and loyalty to Yahweh alone, and to Yahweh's way of justice. This first segment is then the heart of the Sinai covenant, which centers on the integrity of a community's personal allegiance to its religious-political Leader. This allegiance gives orientation and meaning to the eight commandments that follow.

In this first Decalogue segment, Yahweh speaks in first person; in the commands that follow, Yahweh speaks but represented by a third person.[126] The personal, religious character of covenant law, demarcated even from the commandments that follow, is at the heart of the Sinai revolution against all "Hammurabi law," past or present—the Nachfolge Jahweh, the emulation of Yahweh's saving deeds for Israel and the world.

Although the eight stipulations that follow may each have something to offer to the many facets of the subject of capital punishment, perhaps the most relevant is the sixth commandment: "You shall not kill" (RSV, Exod. 20:13; Heb. *raṣḥ*). Some modern English versions translate *raṣḥ* as "murder" (cf. NRSV). Much discussed by scholars, the command is best left generalized.[127] In the Bible the word *raṣḥ* is used of unauthorized killing of another human being, both intentional and unintentional (cf. Deut. 4:42); killing by an avenger (Num. 35:27), and killing in a judicial case authorized by a court (Num. 25:30). It is also used of social situations that deprive widows or orphans of life (Psa. 94:1-6,7; Job 24:1-14).

Since capital punishment and war are authorized by God elsewhere in the Bible, it is usually considered that these are not prohibited by the sixth commandment.[128] However, as stated above, this commandment and the rest are all introduced by 20:2, the "center" of *Yahweh war*;[129] all "secular war" in the Old Testament is unauthorized, and therefore murder (cf. Ezek. 19:3-4; 32:17-32). Though a different vocabulary is used, even a corporate community, a city, may be guilty of murder, unlawful killing before God (cf. Ezek. 22:3-4).

As Dale Patrick says in another setting, "The prohibitions were, from the outset, abstractions intended to apply to a host of different actions. As history went on, new applications were found that were implicit in the original wording although not in the mind of the original author(s)."[130] An example of this might be the book of Jonah, whose author extends a hoary Israelite principle about God's graciousness to Israel to its historic enemy, Nineveh (Jonah 4:2; Exod. 34:6-7; cf. *20:6-7*). Intrinsically, this could mean that the sixth commandment, prohibiting the violation of a horizontal relationship, is to be interpreted and reinterpreted in light of covenant allegiance and loyalty to Yahweh, in the light of the principle, Nachfolge Jahweh (20:2-6). The Sinai Covenant is founded not on Israel's act of war, but upon Yahweh's exclusive grace-act, redemption from Egypt.[131]

THE SINAI COVENANT CODE, EXODUS 20:22–23:19

Following the Decalogue's announcement of the great principles of Sinai law, the covenant code, made up of practical, individual laws[132] and teachings, applies these principles to the individual cases of Israel's earliest communal life.[133] These diverse types of laws and teachings may be classified as two types of material: that formulated by jurists, perhaps from individual legal cases; and that formulated from moral and religious teaching (cf. Exod. 18:20, "statutes" and "instructions").[134]

The block of material formulated from individual legal cases is most like that of the Hammurabi and other Near East law codes.[135] Compared to the Decalogue's declaration of legal principles, the covenant code's name[136] and its present literary position within the covenant inclusion suggests that its intent is to present the specific ways that Israel is to exercise its vocation: a living exemplar, a "holy nation" among the nations (Exod. 19:6).[137]

An outline of the covenant code follows (formulated by Dale Patrick):[138]

I. The Law of the Altar (Exod. 20:23-26)

II. The Judgments (Exod. 21:2-11)
    A. Slavery (Exod. 20:23-26)
    B. Capital Crimes (21:12-17)
    C. Injury to Person by a Person (21:18-27)
    D. Death of Person or Animal by an Animal (21:28-36)
    E. Theft, Damages and Ownership Disputes (22:1-15)
    F. Seduction of Woman not Betrothed (22:16-17)
    G. Capital Offenses Against the Religio-Moral Order
       (22:18-20)

III. Moral Commandments and Duties (Exod. 22: 21–23:9)
    A. Rights of the Weak (22:21-27)
    B. Religious Duties (22:28-31)
    C. Court Process and Dates of Assistance (23:1-9)

IV. Sabbatical Times and the Festival Calendar (23:10-19)
    A. Sabbatical Times (23:10-13)
    B. Festival Calendar (23:14-19)

The entire covenant code is enclosed with laws governing the divine-human relationship (I, IV); such laws are also distributed throughout this enclosure (IIIB). Yahweh spoke this law to the Israelites through the covenant mediator, Moses (20:22), and this personal, religious orientation to the universe provides the structure for justice, for laws that give direction to interhuman relationships.

In contrast, the laws of the Hammurabi Code, like all ancient Near East law collections, are strictly secular: They deal only with interhuman relationships. Borrowing from Yehezkel Kauffman, Shalom M. Paul explains that even though the Hammurabi stele represents law as authorized by the gods, the ultimate source of ancient Mesopotamian law is a transcendent, primordial force on which even the gods depend. Assigned to this realm are the powers of nature, fate, time, magic—powers to which both human and divine beings are subservient. To this impersonal realm may now be added *kittum*, "truth and right," what is established, the sum of immutable truths.[139]

This orientation of covenant law to a personal deity denies the "sovereignty and immutability of the law";[140] only Yahweh is sovereign. From the New Testament perspective, "the Son of man is lord of the Sabbath" (Matt. 12:9). Details of the law are to be interpreted in light of the intent of covenant relationship; because of change in circumstances, technique laws may need to be changed so that they are compatible with the foundation of law, covenant well-being. An example of this change is the book of Deuteronomy, a revised copy of the law as it is given in the first four books (cf. Deut. 17:18).

Thus any separation of religious from moral law is a violation of the very character of covenant law; it is a retreat to the ancient Near East legal codes. These codes are essentially secular; they regulate only interhuman relationships which, in Kauffman's judgment, are based on a presumed impersonal, metaphysical reality. As we shall see, this personal reorientation of covenant law has consequences even for the content of covenant law, in that it favors personal rights above property rights.

A second major difference in the law of the covenant code from the Hammurabi and other Near East codes is the attachment of a "motive-model clause"[141] to individual laws, the clause intimating the divinity's saving act in history.[142] Three such history-related clauses are found in the covenant code:

"You shall not wrong or oppress a resident alien, for you were aliens in the land of Egypt. You shall not abuse any widow or orphan." (Exod. 22:21-22; cf. vv. 23-24)

"You shall not oppress a resident alien, you know the heart of an alien, for you were aliens in the land of Egypt." (Exod. 23:9

"You shall eat unleavened bread for seven days at the appointed time in the month of Abib, for in it you came out of Egypt." (Exod. 23:15)

As noted above, Israel's deliverance from oppression introduces *the covenant anticipation*, which, along with *covenant consummation*, enfolds this entire segment of Sinai law, the Decalogue, and covenant code (Exod. 19:4; 24:3-8). This deliverance also forms the foundation of the Decalogue, Israel's policy law (Exod. 20:2). Finally, in the covenant code (Exod. 20:22–24:8), it is used by Israel's lawgivers to motivate and give direction to certain "technique laws," laws applying commands to specific interhuman relationships!

The "alien" is a foreigner passing through the land or in residence. Due to war and trade, there are many aliens in the ancient Near East. In Israel, they have no attachment to an extended family or tribe and so have only limited political and economic rights. The two interhuman laws protecting the alien, above, are placed in association with laws protecting other disadvantaged persons and justice for the poor.

But while "widow," "orphan," and "poor" are protected also in other Near Eastern law codes, only biblical law gives protection to the alien. In Deuteronomy Israel is commanded, "You shall also love the alien, *for you were aliens in the land of Egypt*" (10:19, emph. added). The Holiness Code says, "When an alien resides with you in your land, you shall not oppress the alien. The alien who resides with you shall be to you "as the citizen among you; you shall love the alien as yourself, *for you were aliens in the land of Egypt*" (Lev. 19:34, emph. added).

If one takes this motive statement seriously, the reason for this unique concern for the alien is a religious one. In a way unlike the other cultures of the ancient Near East, covenant law is oriented toward the personal will and character of a transcendent God rather than toward economic and political concerns, which though important, are secondary. Also, it is obvious that the intent of this motive clause is not merely to protect the disadvantaged, but to propel the disadvantaged toward equal rights with the citizen. It calls for what we moderns name "affirmative action!" And later prophets are not slow to promote such action (cf. Ezek. 47:21-23).

This motive clause is not peripheral but central to Israel's ancient consciousness. It is the reason given here for celebrating Israel's most important festival, the "festival of unleavened bread" and Passover.[143] In the Pentateuch this festival is discussed in Exodus 12-13; 23:15; 34:1;8; Leviticus 23:4-8; Numbers 9:1-15; 28:16-25; 33:3; Deuteronomy 16:1-8 and in the following books of Joshua, Kings, Ezekiel, Ezra, and Chronicles. In post-biblical Judaism it becomes a family festival, celebrating this same act of liberation. In the synoptic Gospels, Jesus reorients and celebrates it with his disciples when he institutes the Last Supper (Matt. 26: 17-29; Mark 14:12-25; Luke 22:7-23). In the book of John, the crucified Jesus is presented as the Pascal lamb.[144] Thus this emphasis of freedom from state slavery forms a trajectory, arching across the Bible, with a major effect upon subsequent history.

Moreover, the motive clauses increase in the later Pentateuchal law codes. While only 16 percent of individual laws in the older Covenant Law Code include this and other motivating clauses (Exod. 20:22–23:33), 51 percent of the laws in the Holiness Code, and 60 percent of the laws in the Deuteronomic Code include such attachments. Thus these three biblical law codes, made up of mainly "technique" or applied law and "teachings" regarding specific cases, are brought into the orbit of the Sinai covenant (19:4-6; 24:1-8) and Decalogue (policy law, 20:1-17).[145] They grow increasingly inward in motivation and progressively theological in modeling. Contrasting to other Near East law, Rifat Sonsino says this of the motive clause:

> It is noteworthy that, unlike biblical laws, no cuneiform law is ever motivated by reference to an historical event, a promise of well-being or, for that matter, a divine will. In fact, in these laws, the deity is completely silent, yielding its place to a human lawgiver, whose main concern is economic rather than religious.[146]

The "resident alien" and other underprivileged persons are given another institutional right in covenant law, the right of Sabbath rest.[147] Like the law of Passover and unleavened bread, motive clauses are attached to this law as it is stated both in the covenant code and the Decalogue. Exodus 23:12: "Six days you shall do your work, but on the seventh day you shall rest, *so that your ox and your donkey may have relief, and your home-born slave and the resident alien may be refreshed*" (emph. added).

This motive clause includes rights for the alien as well as slave, and even animal rights. In the Sabbath proscription of the Decalogue, the motive clause law includes female rights, including females of all classes: the wife who is addressed along with her husband, *you*,[148] the *daughter, male and female slave* (Exod. 20:8-11). Like the covenant code, it includes rights for slave, though more generalized, as well as rights for *livestock* and *resident alien*. While the motive clause of the covenant code reveals its concern for the animals' "relief," and "refreshment" for slave and alien, the Decalogue's motive clause suggests that humans are to pattern their life after Yahweh's creative work, work that includes divine blessing and sanctification of the Sabbath day (Exod. 20:8-11).

Note how the word "holy" begins and ends the commandment (Eng. "holy/consecrate"—Heb. *qdš*). The reader "keeps holy" what Yahweh "has made holy." The deuteronomic version of this Sabbath law has the paradigm of divine redemption instead of that of creation: "Remember that you were a slave in the land of Egypt, and Yahweh your God brought you out from there with a mighty hand and an outstretched arm; therefore Yahweh your God commanded you to keep the Sabbath day" (Deut. 5:15).

This transforming effect of covenant upon covenant code law is not limited to individual laws to which the motive clause is attached. Like an archipelago in the mighty ocean, the motive-model clauses are attached to a few individual laws to form islands, but an oceanographer may suspect that between the islands the ground is rising and may eventually become a continent. Just so, the content of the entire covenant law is reoriented from a Near East impersonal emphasis on economics and protection of property to an emphasis upon personal rights and duties. These are defined not by the state but theologically, which protects the person above property.

Furthermore, while in the Hammurabi Code social classes are specifically named to whom laws favoring the *ruling classes* apply, in the covenant code the opposite is true. No social classes are named, as though all are equal before the law and before Yahweh. While the laws of slavery may be an exception, yet every slave law in the covenant code protects slave rights,

rights of both male and female slaves, turning upside down the Near Eastern preferential treatment of the ruling classes. In ancient Israelite society, whatever social difference there may be, even the indentured slave-woman has rights[149]—*economic* and even *conjugal* rights, protected by covenant law. If these are not respected, she goes out free, "without debt, without payment of money" (Exod. 21:11).

Later deuteronomic law liberalizes this law of the indentured slave even further: Now the law of the slave wife is omitted; this institution is no longer a reality in Israel. Now the law of the slave applies equally to the Hebrew slave man and slave woman, stated at beginning and end of this law (Deut. 15:12, 17). Now the slave-master sends out the Hebrew male "not . . . empty-handed: "Provide liberally out of your flock, your threshing floor and your wine press, thus giving to him some of the bounty with which Yahweh your God has blessed you. *Remember that you were a slave in the land of Egypt, and the Lord your God redeemed you; for this reason I lay this command upon you today"* (Deut. 15:12-17; emph. added).

Hans Boecker comments on Deuteronomy 15:12-15:

> Israel's existence as a people freed from slavery demanded a different view of slavery from that current elsewhere. It is particularly clear in the deuteronomic slave law how law in the Old Testament was interpreted and understood in an increasingly theological way. The awareness that emerged in slave law also impinged on many other areas of life. An essential feature of Deuteronomy is the theologization of older legal prescriptions."[150]

And finally, one deuteronomic law makes all slavery *optional* to the slave:

> "Slaves who have escaped to you from their owners shall not be given back to them. They shall reside with you, in your midst, in any place they choose in any one of your towns, wherever they please; *you shall not oppress them."* (Deut. 23:15-16, emph. added)

Some would argue that this "law of emancipation" is meant to apply only to the indentured or Hebrew slave, but this law uses an unqualified general term (*'ebed*), which in this context should be translated "slave."[151] Those slaves who read or hear this law can make their choice.

Even if judged impractical or "utterly utopian," this published law would raise dangerous slave expectations.[152] One must presume that the institutions of the Hebrew courts were expected to rule on the side of the slave.[153] An Eshnunna slave law rewards the person who brings the fleeing slave back.[154] A Hammurabi law imposes the death penalty on any person who helps the slave to escape, quite opposite from the deuteronomic law.[155] It is unique to ancient Near East law codes that the first laws of the covenant code dealing with interhuman relationships are laws that protect the slave, both male and female (Exod. 21:2-14).[156]

In light of this overwhelming influence of covenant motive clause and covenant worship on biblical law, why do the eight capital cases and the lex talionis, which the covenant code holds in common with Hammurabi Law, resist its forward-thrusting influence?[157] Since in the covenant structure of Sinai law and its motive-model clause it seems evident that the emulation of Yahweh's saving acts for Israel is a major factor in humanizing Israelite law, might one not expect the death penalty (and lex talionis) to be eliminated in covenant law? Might this not be particularly the case since the Hittites came near to eliminating it without benefit of a divine motive-model clause?

But like the ocean archipelago where much of the rising continent is still under water, some places more deeply than others, there remain disappointing laws. That is true for example of the one that some would interpret as designating the slave to be the owner's property (Exod. 21:20-21; cf. Lev. 25:46), and laws with an attached death penalty.

The transforming effect of covenant motive-model clause is not limited to the covenant code and other Pentateuchal law. Although this motive-model clause does not exclude the human death sentence in the ancient Covenant and other Pentateuchal Codes, a number of Old Testament narratives—such as the Cain-Abel (Gen. 4)[158] and Nathan-David accounts (2 Sam. 12)[159] as well as prophetic oracles[160]—substitute for it more benign protective societal and disciplinary measures (Gen. 4; 2 Sam. 12; Hos. 1–3).

These and later developments of the prophets and Gospels in relation to capital punishment are not contradictory to but are what one might expect from covenant law.[161] Rather than the question, "How can these narratives contradict covenant law?," the question may rather be, "Why did the influence of covenant law not eliminate capital punishment and the lex talionis sooner, perhaps even in the earliest covenant code; why does the death penalty persist so long, at least in the law codes?" This question is especially pertinent since Hittite law codes, and Mesopotamian law before Hammurabi's law code do not include the lex talionis.

In worshiping situations, this law was proclaimed at regular intervals to all Israel; and every Israelite was exhorted that by keeping the commandments they were to love and obey God from the heart (cf. Deut. 30:10-13; cf. 6:4-6; Psalm 15). In contrast, Hammurabi's code—though set up in the temple precincts and meant to be read—involves "In the presence of the statue of me, the king of justice. . . ." And its laws deal strictly with interhuman relationships based largely on the threat of human violence.[162]

SUMMARY AND PROSPECT

According to the book of Exodus, the Sinai covenant law is based on the Israelite community's particular experience of divine intervention—the exodus from Egypt and meeting with Yahweh on the mountain. Although Egypt developed no law codes as such, because of the two past centuries of western archaeology, the world now knows that this intervention happened in the context of a body of well developed Near East law. This includes law codes that have been retrieved from the sands of ancient Sumer, Babylon, Assyria, the western Hittites and Ugarit, dating from the twentieth to the sixth centuries B.C. Comparing Sinai law with this Near Eastern body of law reveals that the former has much in common with it, including laws with penalties of capital punishment.

There are major differences in Sinai law however, which must be described as nothing less than revolutionary. The main difference is that while Near East empire law is based on power politics, uniting in the king religion, economics, and the armed services with their threat of pacification and retribution, Sinai law is based on Yahweh's covenant grace: freedom from state slavery, infinite love, and forgiveness, with extremely limited divine retribution.

This covenant grace is both a model and motive for human behavior. It draws into tension Israel's common experience with the case law of the ancient Near East, including the death penalty. Its equal justice accents "affirmative action"—preferential treatment for the disadvantaged such as the slave, alien, widow, and orphan. The relevance of this for today is to realize first of all that such a body of revolutionary law exists as the common heritage of synagogue and church.

We now review the story of Elijah's encounter with God on Sinai-Horeb. Elijah's misguided zeal on Mount Carmel leads to the prophet's request for death in the desert, and lament for the demise of Yahwism at Horeb. But his experience of theophany gives him a new perspective on Sinai law, reconciling him to Yahweh. This experience of theophany leads the way for reflection and decisive action in the historic struggle of "the law and the prophets" to overcome retribution and capital punishment. In that struggle, we will see how these principles of covenant and policy law—divine grace, infinite love and forgiveness (Exod. 20:2-6), so *unlike* the Near East kingship law of retribution—draw into tension the concept of capital punishment which, *like* other Near East law, still remains in covenant technique law with its specific laws of application.

2

On the Mountain with Elijah, and Aftermath: Context and Policy Law Transform Covenant Technique Law
2 Kings 10–Hosea 1-3

Now there was a great wind, so strong that it was splitting mountains and breaking rocks in pieces before Yahweh, but Yahweh was not in the wind; and after the wind an earthquake, but Yahweh was not in the earthquake; and after the earthquake a fire, but Yahweh was not in the fire; and after the fire a sound of sheer silence.
—1 Kings 19:11-12

THE LAW AND THE PROPHETS

Jesus refers to the Hebrew Scriptures as "the law and the prophets" (Matt. 22:40; Luke 16:16). This title, used by the ancient Jews, is in contrast to The Code of Hammurabi which, like similar Near East law codes, associates law primarily with kingship, violent power, the armed services.

Hammurabi, supported by his military power, is called "the king of justice."[163] This Near Eastern reference is similar to our modern concept that associates law with the police force and local, state/provincial, and national courts: "the law and the police."

The Bible differs from all extant Near East historical literature in its overwhelming emphasis on the prophets. While prophecies from the Near East city of Mari, situated close to the traditional place and time of Abraham,[164] have many superficial characteristics of biblical prophecy, they differ from the prophecies of the biblical canon in two major respects: First, they predate the Moses revolution of law described above and therefore know only the power oriented basis for law and city-state: "the law and the king." Their prophetic concern is directed toward the material well-being of the cult (temples, and so forth) and of the kingship, empire, or state, rather than to the biblical prophetic concern—the communal and individual covenant relationship of the people to divinity, to the world, and to one another.

Second, unlike the prophets of the biblical canon, the oracles of these Near Eastern Mari prophets were never gathered up and written down on a scroll to edify and give direction to future generations of the community who might meet similar situations.[165] Evidently, their prophecies were not considered meaningful beyond the immediate situation to which they prophesied. Nor were their prophets given a preeminent place in their social and political order, as happened in Israel according to the biblical canon.[166] Instead of being published on the walls of the palace, temple, or on royal stele, their prophecies were placed in the royal archives and dug up only in the twentieth century A.D. long after their community was dead.

In contrast, the largest segment of the Hebrew Bible consists of The Prophets: The Former Prophets (Josh., Judges, Samuel, Kings),[167] and The Latter Prophets (Isa., Jer., Ezek., and The Book of the Twelve—our minor prophets). Even 1 and 2 Kings are classified as prophetic by the ancient Hebrews and are so recognized by Jesus. The literary structure of these two books simply follows the successive reigns of Israel's and Judah's kings: from King David's death to King Jehoiachin's release from his Babylonian prison (1 Kings 1:1–2 Kings 25:30).

But the literary preoccupation of these books is Yahweh's rule of covenant law, judgment and promise in the crises of Is-

CHART: SUCCESSION OF PROPHETS IN JUDGES–KINGS[168]

Century	Prophet	Text	Spoke to	Message
12th	Deborah	Judg. 4-5	Barak/Israel	Positive
	A Prophet	Judg. 6:7-10	Israel	Negative
11th	Samuel	1 Sam. 3:1-4:1; 25:1	Priest/Israel	Neg/Pos.
	Proph. Company	1 Sam. 10:5-13; 19:20-24		
10th	Nathan	2 Sam. 7:1-17; 1 Kings 1	King/Queen	Pos/Neg.
	Gad	1 Sam. 22:5; 2 Sam. 24:11-25	King	Pos/Neg.
	Ahijah	1 Kings 11:29-40; 14:1-18	Kings	Negative
	Shemaiah	1 Kings 12:22-24	King	Negative
	Man of God	1 Kings 13 2 Kings 23:16-18	King	Negative
	A Prophet	1 Kings 13:11-32	Prophet	Negative
9th	Jehu	1 Kings 16:1-7	King	Negative
	Elijah	1 Kings 17-19; 21 2 Kings 1	Kings/Queen	Negative
	Prophets	1 Kings 18:4, 13; 19: 10, 14		
	A Prophet	1 Kings 20:13-22	King	Positive
	Man of God	1 Kings 20:28-30	King	Positive
	A Prophet	1 Kings 20:35-43	King	Negative
	Micaiah	1 Kings 22	King/Prophets	Negative
	Elisha	2 Kings 2-8; 13:14-21	Kings, and so forth	Pos/Neg.
	Proph. Company	2 Kings 2:3-5, 15-18; 6:1-7		
	Prophet	2 Kings 9:1-13	Kings	Negative
8th	Jonah	2 Kings 14:25	King	Positive
	Isaiah	2 Kings 19-20	King	Pos/Neg.
7th	Prophets	2 Kings 21:10-15	King	Negative
	Huldah	2 Kings 22:14-20	King	Positive
	Prophets	2 Kings 23:2 (Cf. 2 Kings 17:13, 23; 24:2)		

rael's history, as that rule is proclaimed by inspired prophets. From the prophet Samuel to the prophetess Huldah, their negative judgments are directed against those kings who rebel against Yahweh, a rebellion often involving the first and second commandments (1 Sam. 15:22-23; 2 Kings 22:14-20; see chart). Their positive prophecies promote those kings who, though often imperfect, lead their people in repentance and in respect for those institutions that uphold covenant law; the promise of Israel's future lies with them (cf. 2 Sam. 6-7).

These *Former Prophets*, whose oracles are placed within their narrative contexts, and the *Latter Prophets*, whose oracles are gathered together largely without specific narrative contexts, were intended to give religious, social, and political direction for the moment in which they were first spoken. And beyond that, the oracles of both The Former and The Latter Prophets—those gathered together and written down in their respective scrolls, with appropriate editorial additions—were meant to give direction to the covenant people in future, comparable situations (cf. Jer. 36). They illustrate how the prophetic word gives direction to the community, including the king and other officials, especially in times of crisis.

Beginning with Elijah,[169] it is these two points of difference from the Mari prophets that concern us in 1 Kings 19: (1) The Hebrew prophet's experience of the Sinai-Horeb theophany as centering in the "sound of sheer silence" or "prophetic whisper" rather than in its ancient association with wind, earthquake, and fire, natural phenomena associated with the Canaanite god, Baal; and (2) Elijah's own role[170] as prophet leader in Israel's historic religious and political struggle against the Baal-like kingship gods of the Near East.[171] Elijah's revaluation of covenant law, and the Elijah-Elisha struggle against political power gods, continue to be overwhelmingly relevant to the covenant community and to the nations of our own day.

THE BAAL APOSTASY OF
THE OMRIDE DYNASTY AND ELIJAH'S CHALLENGE

The story of the rise and fall of Baal worship and of kingship court prophets in early Israel makes up the "center" of the books of 1 and 2 Kings (1 Kings 16:23–2 Kings 12).[172] In the longer Deuteromistic History, this segment on Baal apostasy reaches "the second and absolute high point on the negative scale of the history of the Northern Kingdom. With the Jehu revolution the sinfulness of the North was seemingly again reduced to its 'normal' measure, for even Jehu continued in 'the sins of Jeroboam,'"[173] first king of the Northern Kingdom.

Jeroboam's sin, which even Jehu continues, is Israel's first though somewhat lesser "high point on the negative scale." He adjusts Yahweh worship to promote his own political goals, meaning that he threatens the theopolitical unity of Yahwism by establishing official places of worship apart from Jerusalem (1 Kings 12:26-33; cf. 1 Kings 15:26; 16:2, 19, 26, 31-32; 21:20-22; 22:52).

This Baal apostasy is promoted by the Israelite dynasty founded by the army commander, Omri (Kings Omri, Ahab, Ahaziah, Joram, 842 B.C.-747 B.C.), and by Jezebel, the Baal-worshiping wife of king Ahab (1 Kings 16:15-33). By a marriage of diplomacy of Ahab's daughter to king Jehoram of Judah, Baal becomes a threat even to Judah (2 Kings 11; cf. 8:16-18). The back of this Baal movement is broken by a people's movement instigated by the prophet Elijah on Mount Carmel (1 Kings 18).[174] He is assisted at the end by his disciple Elisha and an unnamed member of his prophetic school, who touched off the Jehu revolution (2 Kings 9).[175]

After fleeing before the martial power of King Ahab because he had threatened him with a devastating drought (1 Kings 17), prophet Elijah returns to Israel to call together the traditional covenant-making assembly of all Israel (1 Kings 18:20-46; cf. Josh. 24:1-28; Deut. 31:9-13). There he successfully challenges the worship of Baal and the leadership of his prophets.

It is noteworthy that Elijah chooses for this contest not an ancient traditional center of Israel such as Shechem, or even its capital Samaria, but the frontier region of Mount Carmel.[176] Though beleaguered and driven by Ahab and Jezebel both to the East and to the North (1 Kings 17:1-3, 8-10), Elijah adopts no retreating, citadel strategy. He challenges royal apostasy on the frontier, where, in Israel's history, Baalism is likely the strongest and where covenant assemblies are without precedent (Exod. 19:1, 2, 17; Josh. 24:1; 1 Sam. 10:17; and so forth; cf. Deut. 31:9-13). There Elijah defeats the Baal prophets in an ordeal by fire, and the assembly chooses Yahweh as their God: "Yahweh, he is God" (1 Kings 18:39 RSV).

To seal the success of this contest, Elijah says to the people, "'Seize the prophets of Baal; do not let one of them escape.' Then they seized them; and Elijah brought them down to the Wadi Kishon, and killed them there" (1 Kings 18:40). The Baal prophets violate the first commandment; and Elijah administers the retribution prescribed by technique law (cf. Exod. 22:20)—not without legal precedent, yet without a direct command from Yahweh.

CONFRONTATION AT HOREB: YAHWEH'S QUESTION, ELIJAH'S COMPLAINT, 1 KINGS 19:9-10[177]

But Elijah discovers that the death of these Baal prophets does not end the conflict. When Jezebel is told of their massacre, she threatens him with death (1 Kings 19). Again, Elijah runs for his life, this time not to the east and north, but to the south (cf. 1 Kings 17). This flight, motivated by fear and not at the command of Yahweh (cf. 17:2-3, 8-9; 18:1),[178] is transformed by the word of an angel into a pilgrimage of forty days and forty nights, linking this event with the experience of Moses on Sinai/Horeb (cf. Exod. 24:17; 33:17-23; 1 Kings19:12, 9-13).

On the mountain, God puts the question, and Elijah responds with his complaint:

> "What are you doing here, Elijah?" [Elijah] answered, "I have been very zealous for Yahweh, the God of hosts, for the Israelites have forsaken your covenant, thrown down your altars, and killed your prophets with the sword. I alone am left, and they are seeking my life, to take it away." And he said, "Go out, and stand on the mountain before Yahweh, for Yahweh is about to pass by." *Now there was a great wind, so strong that it was splitting mountains and breaking rocks in pieces before Yahweh, but Yahweh was not in the wind; and after the wind an earthquake, but Yahweh was not in the earthquake; and after the earthquake a fire, but Yahweh was not in the fire; and after the fire a sound of sheer silence. When*

Elijah heard it, he wrapped his face in his mantle and went out and stood at the entrance of the cave. Then there came a voice to him, that said, "What are you doing here, Elijah?" He answered, "I have been very zealous for Yahweh the God of hosts; for the Israelites have forsaken your covenant, thrown down your altars, and killed your prophets with the sword. I alone am left, and they seek my life, to take it away." (1 Kings 19:9-14, emph. added)

Baalism has won, says Elijah; Yahwism is dead!

In this text, God's question and Elijah's complaint are stated word for word at both the beginning and the end of Elijah's experience with theophany (19:9-10, [11-12], 13-14; cf. above, Exod. 19:4-6; 24:3-8). Literarily, this repetition forms an "inclusion" or envelope structure,[179] here indicating the concern that the theophany at the center is meant to address.[180]

From the immediate literary context, Yahweh's question has two answers: Elijah is there because, fearing Jezebel, he flees into the wilderness wishing to die; and he is there because Yahweh's angel diverts his flight to the desert into a pilgrimage to Mount Horeb—to confrontation, reorientation, and a new possibility (1 Kings 19:1-9a). From a larger literary perspective this sacred space and event may designate I Kings 19 as the climax of the Deuteronomistic History, and Elijah as a second Moses (1 Kings 19:8; cf. 8:9; Deut. 5:2; Exod. 3:1). From this literary point of view, it redefines for Elijah what the Sinai theophany of Moses is about, and it is decisive in determining the way to Yahweh's future triumph over Baal.

Elijah's complaint is directed against Yahweh because of divine inaction to support the prophet. His life, because of past zeal for Yahweh is now threatened, as the "Israelites have forsaken *your covenant,* thrown down *your* altars, killed *your* prophets" (emph. added.) "And," he continues, "*I* alone am left, and they are seeking *my* life (cf. 18:13, 18, 22, 30, emph. added).

By forsaking covenant and breaking down Yahweh's altars, Israel is no longer accepting law within the context of Yahweh's covenant relationship and worship but instead, is substituting Baal's kingship power context for law and worship (cf. above, the discussion of Exod. 19-24, and Deut. 5:1-25a; 17:14-

20, esp. vv. 18-20). And as for the prophets, guardians of Israel's covenant law, Israel's king and Jezebel have killed them, and now threaten the life of Elijah. King, rather than prophet, is in process of becoming the central "guardian" of a power-oriented law like that of other cultures of the ancient Near East (cf. 1 Kings 21, esp. vv. 2, 3).[181]

It is noteworthy that our modern state law compares not with Israelite covenant law, but with the power-oriented law of the other ancient Near East states! Only synagogue and church can provide a prophetic covenant context for law; and only as we acknowledge this objective covenant orientation of Sinai law can we understand what Elijah's confrontation on Sinai/Horeb is about.

And what has Elijah been doing? As guardian of Yahweh's law, he has been "very zealous for Yahweh God of hosts;" he has killed 450 of Baal's prophets (1 Kings 18:19, 40).

> "In the biblical tradition, human acts of zeal punished idolatrous violations of God's right to exclusive allegiance from Israel. As expressed in the First Commandment, God is a jealous/zealous God who requires the allegiance of the people. Because God's holiness will not tolerate idolatry or other violations against the covenant (Exod. 20:5; Deut. 5:9), God will punish the whole nation for such offenses, unless someone acts on behalf of God—zealous with God's jealous anger—to kill or root out the offenders."[182]

Elijah's complaint is against this holy, zealous God: "You ask, 'What am I doing here, Almighty One?' I have been very zealous for you (cf. Exod. 22:20). But where have you been for me, Yahweh God of hosts?" The biblical scholar F. M. Cross says that the *Yahweh of hosts* was originally "the epithet *par excellence* of the divine warrior in Israel."[183]

In a later narrative, this Warrior God responds to Elijah's prayer by raining down fire from heaven to consume the troops of Ahaziah, son of king Ahab (2 Kings 1:9-12; cf. Luke 9:54). On Mount Carmel, Elijah prays down fire to consume the sacrifice; but when he kills the prophets of Baal he acts entirely on his own—not entirely out of line with a certain Israelite tradition perhaps, but with no prayer and no command from Yahweh (18:40; cf. vv. 36-38). "I was very zealous on Mount

Carmel," Elijah complains; "but where were you, O Zealous One—Yahweh God of hosts" (cf. Exod. 20:5; Deut. 5:9)?

"Now the reason for Elijah's trip to Horeb is clear. He has not come to Horeb to do Yahweh's will; rather, he is still fleeing from Jezebel and seeking Yahweh's pity (cf. v. 40). As Elijah's words make plain, the angel's twofold feeding of the prophet did not shore up Elijah's courage and renew his trust in the power of Yahweh as the God of life. Rather, he seems as despondent as he was in 19:3-4. He has come to Horeb to bemoan *the downfall of Yahweh*, the slaying of Yahweh's prophets, and his own sorry fate as one marked for death. It is as if the victory in ch.18 had never taken place."[184]

THEOPHANY AT HOREB: THREE
NEGATIVES AND A WHISPER, 1 KINGS 19:11-14A

The Warrior God, Yahweh (cf. Exod. 15:4), responds to Elijah's complaint by reminding him what Sinai law is like in its covenant context.[185] Although the people at Sinai "witnessed the thunder and lightning . . . and the mountain smoking" (Exod.20:18), natural events common in Near Eastern and Canaanite theophanies,[186] prophet Elijah is not to confuse the character of the Warrior God Yahweh with the nature of the warrior god Baal.

As "the paradigmatic warrior god"[187] in Canaanite myth, Baal is identified with the storm—the "strong wind," "the earthquake," the "fire." Yahweh, however, is not in these phenomena of nature, as emphasized by three negatives (Heb. *lo*, 19:11-12), but is identified with divine communication, a positive: "and after the fire a still small voice" (RSV translation of *qol demoma daqqa*), or "a sound of sheer silence" (NRSV). The first possibility denotes divine communication; the second, the prophet's contemplative receptivity, his or her ability to intuit Yahweh's communication.[188]

Although not entirely adequate, Georg Fohrer's comment on this theophany is instructive:

The Being of Yahweh is not depicted with symbols of storm, earthquake and fire, which symbolize the sudden and frightening power of the holy and unapproachable God that scorns all efforts of self-defense by man. The divine being is rather described by the gentle stillness of the breeze. [Thus] there is a turning from the God of war and battles to the God whose being is not revealed in terrifying outbursts, but who can be compared to the gentle stillness of the breeze.[189]

This statement should not be interpreted merely in terms of "inward spiritualization," but in terms of Yahweh war, Yahweh's deliverance of Israel from Egypt, Yahweh's saving act celebrated as the basis for covenant law (Exod. 19-24).[190]

In my opinion, the comment of Jorg Jeremias supports that of Fohrer, but goes beyond it by regarding the theophany as polemical in relation to Israel's environment, other Near East religious cultures:[191]

Were there circles in Israel which spoke of the coming of Yahweh in the "still small voice (of the wind)," and which rejected the link, often made in Israel, between Yahweh and the destructive forces of nature, because, in Israel's religious environment, the manifestation of the gods was usually just so linked with them? In this case it was not a more refined conception of God which characterized these circles, but their opposition to equating the religion of Yahweh with the religions of the world around. The polemic against *the world around would necessarily lead to a polemic against Israel's own religious tradition*. At the time of Elijah such a polemic would have been quite conceivable.[192]

Even early biblical poetry distinguishes Israel as "a people living alone, and not reckoning itself among the nations" (Num. 23:9). As Martin Noth so well wrote,

Yet despite all [its] historical connections and possibilities for comparison, 'Israel' still appears a stranger in the world of its own time, a stranger wearing the garments and behaving in the manner of its age, yet separate from the world it lived in, not merely in the sense that every historical reality has its own individual character, and therefore an element of uniqueness, but rather at the center of the history of Israel we encounter phenomena for which there is no parallel at all elsewhere, not because material for comparison has not yet come to light but because so far as we know, such things have simply never happened elsewhere.[193]

Elijah's accusation against Israel and Yahweh would suggest that either Elijah is right, that Yahweh has failed in this conflict against Baal, or that Elijah is in need of a major revaluation of what Sinai covenant law is about. In contrast to the Baal-like warrior god(s) of the ancient Near East, it is because the Warrior Yahweh is dominant in Hebrew tradition that Yahweh's prophet must know this: *Human violence as the basis for Near Eastern law is displaced in Sinai law*—indeed, in the entire Bible, from Sinai-Horeb,194 to the Plains of Moab,195 to the Sermon on the Mount,196 there is no kingship law code—only prophetic covenant codes.197

The "center" of biblical law and its theophany is covenant love rather than human violence and retribution. The sovereign, prophetic covenant God Yahweh of the Sinai theophany is not to be confused with the kingship god Baal.

By Yahweh's response of theophany to his lament, Elijah must know that because Yahweh is different from Baal at the point of *power politics*, the prophet like Moses must suffer (cf. Exod. 33:12-22). Because Yahweh is a warrior, this Holy One will not defend Elijah against Jezebel's wrath with a powerful human army.

This disclosure of theophany, answer to Elijah's lament, is an intimation that trust and suffering (18:4) rather than political violence is the inherent characteristic of the prophetic office. Trust and suffering love are intrinsic even to Israelite kingship as it obeys the prophetic voice (cf. Deut. 17:14-20); indeed they are intrinsic also to the vocation of all Israel as "a treasured possession and priestly kingdom" of the covenant God to whom the "whole earth" belongs (Exod. 19:5-6). Elijah's Sinai theophany is a major pivot in the ragged trajectory from Moses toward the suffering servant (Isa. 42–53[198]), a servant commissioned to bring forth Yahweh's justice and torah "to the nations" by nonviolent proclamation (Isa. 42:1-4):

> "Here is my servant, whom I uphold, my chosen, in whom my soul delights; I have put my spirit upon him; he will bring forth *justice* to the nations. He will not cry or lift up

his voice, or make it heard in the street; a bruised reed he will not break, and a dimly burning wick he will not quench; he will faithfully bring forth *justice*. He will not grow faint or be crushed until he has established *justice* in the earth; and the coastlands wait for his *teaching*" (*torah*; emph. added).

ELIJAH'S COMMISSION:
THREE ANOINTINGS AND A PROMISE, 1 KINGS 19:15-18

John Gray comments, "The significance of the theophany to Elijah at Horeb has been taken to be the revelation that the violent measures adopted by Elijah at Carmel were not the methods Yahweh wanted of his servants." Gray does not accept this interpretation.[199] Indeed, this logical interpretation may be qualified somewhat, though not essentially, by the fact that the *still small voice* of prophecy is soon to touch off an even greater bloodbath than that on Carmel—the "blood of Jezreel," a bloodbath that must wait for its own retribution, one prophesied by the prophet Hosea a century later (Hos. 1:4-5).[200]

Yahweh's "still small voice"[201] tells Elijah to anoint three persons: Hazael as king of Syria; Jehu, king Joram's army commander, as king of Israel; and Elisha as Elijah's prophetic successor. Yahweh then explains, "Whoever escapes from the sword of Hazael,[202] Jehu shall kill; and whoever escapes from the sword of Jehu, Elisha shall kill. Yet I will leave seven thousand in Israel who have not bowed the knee to Baal" (1 Kings 19:15-18).

But Elijah follows through with none of this violence; he designates only Elisha as his successor (1 Kings 19:19-21). Hazael's Syrian coup is touched off later by Elijah's disciple, Elisha (2 Kings 8:7-15).[203] And Jehu's Israelite coup, though prompted by Elisha, is touched off by a member of Elisha's prophetic company (2 Kings 9:1-13). And as far as we know, Elisha kills no one. Elijah throws "his mantle over him" (19:19), and later he is designated head of the "company of the prophets" (2 Kings 2:9-12, 15); as such, he is recognized leader of the "seven thousand in Israel . . . that have not bowed to Baal."

How is this variance between command and execution to be explained—with its transfers from Elijah to Elisha, then to an unknown member of the prophetic school? There may be several possible explanations. But I suggest that different literary sources[204] may reflect tensions within the prophetic party—perhaps even within the heart of canonical prophets and others in Israel—about the appropriateness of direct participation in retributive violence, given the unique nature of Yahweh as warrior.

Note the narrative of the unknown member of the school of the prophets who heartlessly enforced the ban against the Aramaean king Benhadad, countermanding the merciful decision of the magnanimous king of Israel toward his enemy (1 Kings 20:23-43). Compare this with the two narratives of Elisha's compassionate healing of the enemy: the story of Naaman, Aramean army commander (2 Kings 5:1-19), and of that prophet's gracious hospitality to the trapped Aramean army which, after a feast, he then sent home, refusing to enforce the ban (2 Kings 6:8-23). The tension we noted in the character of covenant law—retribution toward individual deviant covenant members (Exod. 21:23-25) versus Yahweh's saving mercy of Israel from oppression and slavery (Exod. 20:2)—is becoming more inward, even divisively so.

After eliding the theophany from the original text (1 Kings 19:11b-12),[205] Ernst Würthwein regards Elijah's commission (1 Kings 19:15-18) as the pivot of this chapter, thus interpreting the "pivot" as the canonical prophets' unreserved justification of Jehu's revolution, and the promise of the saved remnant as a lesson for post-exilic Israel.[206] But J. J. Stamm, correctly I think, regards the theophany as the pivot (1 Kings 19:11b-12),[207] and relates its fourth element, "the still small voice," to the fourth pronouncement of the commission, the promise (19:15-18): "Yet I will leave seven thousand in Israel, all the knees that have not bowed to Baal, and every mouth that has not kissed him." Stamm writes,

"The continued existence of the people of God depends on these seven thousand. Therefore they represent *the real object of Yahweh's activity, the sphere where he is present.* By contrast, Elijah's spectacular tasks represent only transitional stages, acts of judgment which forward this aim. *Yahweh is also the originator of these, but they are not the sphere of his ac-*

tual presence. Thus the encounter with God, with its four elements is a preparation for the future career of the prophet, particularly with regard to the seven thousand whom he himself can neither bring together nor protect. He must simply believe that they will be there and the fourth element of the theophany is a guarantee of this."[208]

In defense of Stamm's concept, that the sphere of the divine presence is present in Yahweh's salvation activity rather than in judgment, I would maintain that Elijah's experience of theophany speaks not *in general* about God, judgment and salvation, but *specifically* to Elijah about *how the theophanic experience of Moses and the people at Mount Sinai is to be interpreted.* Although the people did indeed witness "the thunder and lightning . . . and were afraid," they are told not to fear for that is only for their testing (Exod. 20:18).

The real meaning of Sinai is not death, but life in the divine Presence: "You have seen what *I did to the Egyptians,* and how I bore you on eagles wings and *brought you to myself*" in covenanted relationship (Exod. 19:4, emph. added). In the Sinai experience of theophany, Israel experienced Yahweh's covenantal Presence, which Egypt in judgment did not experience—but that even in judgment may be on the way toward this divine goal for Pharaoh's future (cf. Exod. 7:4-5).[209]

In my opinion, the apostle Paul is correct in interpreting Elijah's experience at Horeb when he criticizes Elijah's lament:

> "Do you not know what the Scripture says of Elijah, how he pleads with God against Israel? 'Lord, they have killed your prophets, they have demolished your altars; I alone am left, and they are seeking my life.' But what is the divine reply to him? 'I have kept for myself seven thousand who have not bowed the knee to Ba'al.'" (Rom. 11:2b-4).[210]

Instead of interceding with Yahweh for the people, one of the prophet's prescribed tasks,[211] Elijah accuses them. Elijah is not on the side of Yahweh's mercy for Israel but on the side of divine judgment—"wind, earthquake, and fire" (cf. Gen. 18:22-32).

Some would say that Yahweh's theophany does not lead Elijah to repentance, that he is unchanged by it.[212] They would see Elijah's commission to initiate divine retribution (1 Kings 19:15-17), rather than the divine whisper of theophany (19:11-14), as the pivot of this chapter. But after the theophany, Elijah no longer considers himself indispensable—in the place of Yahweh. He trusts the Whisper, the Silence; he throws his mantle over his successor, and with his work unfinished, he is prepared to leave the scene.

While an exit in a chariot may seem more fitting for an emperor than for a prophet, especially in the light of a theophany which has denigrated the symbols of violent power, perhaps here the chariot becomes a symbol of promise: that the prophetic whisper, while not violent, will nevertheless be effective on the plane of history. (See Hosea 14:3 and Isaiah 31:1 for a prophetic critique of advanced weaponry, the military horse, and chariotry.)

The experience of Elijah clarifies the meaning of Sinai, this time at the covenant center, rather than the stormy periphery: The character of Yahweh's own being as warrior God is represented by suffering prophet, in contrast to the warrior god, Baal, as represented by warrior king (1 Kings 1:9-18). Now follows the struggle as to how this clarification is to be implemented in the tumultuous religious-political conflict on the concrete stage of history—in the arena of collective and individual covenant breaches and violations of technique law (which must be taken seriously in any biblical concept of grace).

Is retribution and death by the sword of Hazael and Jehu the means and goal of this climax of the Deuternomistic History?[213] No! Its means and goal is repentance as at the assembly on Mount Carmel (1 Kings 18:36-39)—salvation and life as a portent of a different (eschatological) level, portrayed by the pivot of theophany and its attendant commission with promise (19:11-13, 18)! This new life is signaled by the prophetic career of Elisha to which we will now give our attention.

CHARIOTS OF FIRE
AND HORSES OF FIRE, 2 KINGS 2:12–13:14

First I will examine the promise of the "seven thousand" (19:18), as its fulfillment is portrayed in the Elisha narratives (1

Kings 19:19-21; 2 Kings 2:1–13:21) and in a few of their antecedents in the Elijah narratives. Elijah, who complains that "I alone am left" (1 Kings 19:10, 14), discovers that he is quite dispensable, though he is removed in regal splendor. "Walking and talking" with his servant Elisha as they journey toward the Jordan, "the two of them" are suddenly separated by "a chariot of fire and horses of fire" (2 Kings 2:11).

His servant Elisha, never anointed so far as we know, has been visibly cloaked in Elijah's authority (1 Kings 19:19) and inwardly equipped with a "double share" of his spirit (2 Kings 2:9-10). Perhaps traumatized by this spectacular—though expected—separation on this final walk with his old master, Elisha "keeps watching and crying out, 'Father, father! The chariots of Israel and its horsemen!" (2 Kings 2:12).

This cry, acknowledging Yahweh as Warrior and arising out of this visionary experience with Elijah (a vision later shared with his own servant in a spectacular encounter with an Aramean army; 2 Kings 6:15-19) will be heard again at the death of Elisha, this time from the mouth of a weeping king, Joash of Israel (2 Kings 13:14-15). It thus forms an inclusio around the stories of Elisha's ministry. As an inclusio, it first points backward to define the vocation of Elijah; at the end of Elisha's ministry it points backward again to define the vocation of Elisha. For the deuteronomic historian(s), these prophetic narratives, rather than narratives of human kings and conquerors, are the stories of the movers and shakers of human history.

The cry *"Father, father! The chariots of Israel and its horsemen"* acknowledges dependence upon and trust in Yahweh, God of the repentant Elijah (1 Kings 18:19; 19:10, 14), as the defining characteristic of the ministries of both of these prophets (cf. Exod. 20:2; 2 Kings 6:11-23; Isa. 7:3-9; 14:28-32; 28:14-42). Yahweh is a warrior. But this war, while quite carnal in that it is fought on the plane of Israel's violent history, amid the nations, is nevertheless Yahweh's war, a "holy war." Like the battle against Pharaoh at the Sea, it is fought not with carnal weapons but with Yahweh's "chariots of fire and horses of fire."

ELISHA, SHEPHERD TO THE "SEVEN THOUSAND"

The beginning of the "Elisha Biography," unique in the Old Testament, is much like the Jesus stories of the Gospels and is perhaps the model for those stories. After the company of prophets accepts Elisha's leadership, the account begins with two incidents then is interrupted with an evaluation of a king's reign and Elisha's involvement in a war with Moab. The series continues with four pastoral narratives, broadens out with a story of Elisha's pastoral relationship with Israel's enemy, and so carries on throughout the cluttered biography. Contrary to the enclosing warrior image "chariots and horses of fire," these narratives are not primarily about marauding foreign armies or the mayhem of Jehu's judgments. Instead, seven community-building portraits portray the prophet as shepherd-pastor to this new community of the "seven thousand."

The community itself is not the result of Elijah's labors. It arises, unrecognized by him, out of the dry ground of the prophet's lament, not as the product of sex and zealous violence, akin to that of Jezebel's Baal religion (1 Kings 18:3-4, 13, 40; 19:1-2), but the fruition of the divine "whisper," the "sheer silence" of Yahweh's creative word.[214]

In the first community-building portrait, Elisha meets the civic needs of Jericho. The "people of the city" acknowledge that environmentally, the "location of the city is good . . . ; but the water is bad, and the land is unfruitful." Through the word of Elisha,[215] "Yahweh makes this water wholesome; from now on neither death nor miscarriage shall come from it" (2 Kings 2:19-22).

The second portrait is one of judgment.[216] On his itinerary from Jericho to Bethel, to Mount Carmel and back to Samaria, Elisha curses "small boys" who "came out of the city of Bethel." Forty-two boys are "mauled" by two she-bears (2 Kings 2:24-25; cf. Matt. 19:19-21). In light of the Bible's concern for disadvantaged children, this curse is difficult to accept from a prophet. Given the many human protests against divine judgments in the Bible, certainly our protest is appropriate here (cf. Ezek. 11:13; Acts 5:1-5).

The third portrait is that of a poor widow who is a "member of the company of prophets" (2 Kings 4:1-7). She presents to

Elisha her dilemma: "Your servant my husband is dead; and you know that your servant feared Yahweh, but a creditor has come to take my two children slaves." The anomaly is that covenant members are not to be slaves of one another, for they are slaves of Yahweh, the God whom they fear (cf. Exod. 21: 2-11; Deut. 15:18; Lev. 25:39-43).

Perhaps because of economic change and religious and social breakdown as witnessed by the narrative of Naboth's vineyard, the old institutions of jubilee and debt forgiveness are inadequate to restrain and transform Israel's economic predators. So Elisha provides the widow with a capital resource that she and her children can sell, not merely to pay off her husband's debt but to provide social security for her and their future. Life for this family includes freedom from slavery and from death due to poverty, much beyond what she had requested.

A fourth portrait. While Elisha passes through Shunem on his way toward Mount Carmel, a wealthy woman and her husband provide him with hospitality: a regular meal and a new room with "a bed, a table, a chair, and a lamp." When he offers to reward her with "a word spoken on your behalf to the king or to the commander of the army," she declines. "I live among my own kinfolk."[217] Perhaps she means that her own responsibilities and security are defined not by king and army commander, but by the more ancient arrangement of the security of prophet and kinfolk group that precedes and to some extent may follow the administration of Solomon, after the kingdom has been divided (cf. 1 Kings 4:7-19).[218]

When the woman says she has no need of these gifts, he offers her the promise of a son, even though her husband is an old man. When the son dies, Elisha restores him (2 Kings 4:8-37), much as Elijah formerly has restored the son of the widow at Sidon. Thus this prophetic climax of the deuteronomistic historian emphasizes resurrection and life—at the beginning of the Elijah-Elisha cycle, (1 Kings 17:8-24), toward its middle (2 Kings 4:17-30), and at the end where even to touch the bones of a dead prophet gives life and resurrection (13:21).[219]

The fifth portrait is of Elisha when he returns to Gilgal and is again with the company of the prophets. They put on a large pot to make a stew out of herbs that have been gathered. When the stew is found poisonous and inedible, the prophet purifies it and the people eat it without harm (1 Kings 4:38-41). Again the prophet is life-giving.

A sixth portrait may be compared to those narratives of Jesus feeding the five and four thousand (2 Kings 4:42-44; cf. Matt. 14:13-21; 15:32-39). Food has been donated to the "man of God," but it is insufficient for the "hundred people." Nevertheless, when the prophet commands his servant to set it before them "they ate and had some left."

The poverty of the "company of the prophets" is again apparent in a seventh portrait. While communally involved in building a new place to live, one of them loses a borrowed ax head as he hews down logs at the Jordan. Elisha retrieves the ax head by making it float; the builder "reached out his hand and took it" (2 Kings 6:1-7). The building is assured and the distress of the impoverished community is relieved.

In addition to these stories that deal with the everyday needs of the people, there are two other miracle narratives in which Elisha is involved with Israelite and Aramean kings, army commanders, and raiding parties. Both stories breathe a spirit of universalism and compassion. In the first, the Aramean army commander, Naaman, is healed from a serious skin disease (2 Kings 5:1-27). Naaman's wife, her Israelite slave girl, Elisha, and his servant Gahazi are all involved in this healing story of international relations. In the end, Naaman the Aramean becomes one of the "seven thousand" who worship only Yahweh (2 Kings 5:17:18).

A second compassionate story involves the Aramaian king and another raid. By a miracle, Elisha entraps the raiders in Samaria. He refuses to apply the ban, however, and after feeding the party, sends them on their way. The story ends, "And the Arameans no longer came raiding into the land of Israel" (2 Kings 6: 8-23). History is changed—though not by much.

Compared to the economic and political pressures of the ancient Near East that thrust themselves at the Omride-Ahab dynasty, these stories seem inconsequential. But they are the whisper of the Sinai/Horeb theophany. The editor(s) of the Deuteronomistic History places them up front in the Elisha cycle; in the biblical narrative they are examples of the prophets' impact on their world.

The mayhem that surrounds and follows them nearly overwhelms these stories. But they are not meant to be read in isolation; they are to be read where they are placed, at the cutting edge of a turbulent international history. Without them the wind, earthquake and fire of that history are

> but a walking shadow, a poor player
> That struts and frets his hour upon the stage
> And then is heard no more: it is a tale
> Told by an idiot, full of sound and fury
> Signifying nothing.[220]

But with these stories, even the chaos is a portent that "the whole creation has been groaning in labor pains until now" (Rom. 8:22).

ELISHA AND THE THREE NEGATIVES: WIND, EARTHQUAKE, AND FIRE

But we are still left with the discussion of the three negatives. To understand the Jehu revolution, one must see it in the light both of the Sinai/Horeb *whisper* as its commission is effected in the birthing of the 7000 (1 Kings 19), and of the attendant *wind, earthquake, and fire,* Israel's violent political response to domestic and international pressures. Israel's most serious military involvement at the mid-ninth century B.C. is with Damascus,[221] although that capital also forms an important buffer for Israel against the westward advance of the Assyrian empire, into much of the next century.[222] In the Aramean war stories of his "biography," Elisha is twice featured as a prophet in the defense of Israel against Aram (6:8-23; 6:24-7:20).

But Elisha is not overly patriotic. He is not power oriented, but morally and spiritually oriented—rule of Yahweh oriented; like Jesus in this respect. He partly carries out the first directive of Elijah's commission at Mount Horeb by going to "Damascus when King Benhadad of Aram was ill" (2 Kings 8:7; cf. 1 Kings 19:15). There he weeps as he incites Hazael, a high court official in Damascus, to usurp the Aramean throne (2 Kings 8:7-15). Elisha knows what he is doing; and Israel will remember Hazael as one of its most brutal enemies (cf. 2 Kings 10:32-33). Elijah's commission is designed as Yahweh's judgment against Israel—wind, earthquake, fire—the asymmetrical opposite to the whisper, the whisper that calls into being the "seven thousand" who do not bow to the Canaanite war god, Baal.[223] They who worship Baal shall die by Baal, the Canaanite storm and war god.[224]

But just how far does the prophet involve himself with these idolatrous powers? Besides enticing the foreigner Hazael to usurp the Damascus throne, Elisha also is involved in the second directive of Elijah's commission: "You shall also anoint Jehu, son of Nimshi, as king over Israel" (1 Kings 19:16; cf. 2 Kings 9). So, besides the Damascus revolt, Elisha sets off a second violent revolution when he instructs "a member of the company of prophets" to go to Israel's battlefront at Ramoth-Gilead where king "Joram and all Israel stand guard . . . against King Hazael of Aram" (2 Kings 9:14-15; cf. 8:28-29).

From an archaeological inscription recently unearthed at Tel Dan, "Jehu appears to have executed his revolution not under the protection of Assyria but rather with the support of Hazael, the king of Aram"[225]—whom Elisha earlier had enticed to usurp the Damascus throne! This conspiracy happens while Israel's "King Joram had returned to be healed in Jezreel of the wounds that the Arameans had inflicted on him, when they fought against King Hazael of Aram at Ramoth-Gilead" (1 Kings 9:15a).

Are Elijah and Elisha traitors to their country, on the side of Samaria's enemy, Damascus? A century later, the prophet Amos is accused of such behavior: "Amaziah, priest of Bethel, sent" to the king of Israel, "saying, 'Amos has conspired against you in the very center of the house of Israel" (Amos 7:10).

Agreeing with the priest of Bethel's evaluation of Amos, H. Winkler, a German scholar of the ancient Near East, wrote in 1901 that the great Hebrew prophets of the eighth century B.C—Isaiah and others—are agents of the Assyrian Empire; their political directives come from Nineveh.[226] Like Amos defending himself against the priest Amaziah, Isaiah and other eighth-century prophets understand themselves quite differently than foreign agents; they are not traitors (Amos 7: 14-17; Isa. 6–8). But they are not typical patriots either;[227] they speak from the perspective of the theophany, the rule of God.

JEHU'S BLOOD BATH AT JEZREEL, 2 KINGS 9:1–10:31

As noted above, the wounded king Joram, Ahab's son, has retired for healing from the battlefront to his palace in Jezreel. There Jehu, the rebel army officer, pursues and shoots him through the heart with an arrow. Jehu's military party also pursues and kills Ahaziah king of Judah, Joram's confederate in the war against Aram. As Jehu initiates the fatal attack, Joram calls to his confederate, "Treason, Ahaziah!" (*mirmah*, 2 Kings 9:23). From the perspective of the prophetic tradition of Yahweh, King of Israel, and Omri's dynasty, however, who is guilty of treason here (cf. Isa. 8:11-15)?

Modern commentators, Mordechai Cogan and Hayim Tadmor, write about Omri's dynasty:

> The story of Jehu's overthrow of the dynasty of Omri is related in the longest sustained narrative in 2 Kings; its fifty-nine verses (9:1-6, 10b-28, 30-37; 101-27) grip the reader with the same intensity which must have motivated the main protagonist. The drama unfolds in a series of short scenes, and action, not words, carries Jehu from the army camp facing Ramoth-Gilead to the palace at Jezreel and from there to the temple of Baal in Samaria. By alternating perspectives from time to time, the narrator achieves a fuller characterization of his actors, thus, the army commanders pass judgment upon the prophetic "madman" (9:11); the lookout on the tower recognizes Jehu by his wild driving (9:20); Jezebel primps herself before meeting her certain fate (9:30); the grisly pile of heads effectively intimidates the crowd at the gate of Jezreel (10:7–10). A single narrator, working under the impact of the dramatic turn of events, was undoubtedly responsible for these vivid descriptions.[228]

Cogan and Tadmor state that one basic theme "unites all aspects of the narrative: Jehu's deeds against the House of Ahab fulfill YHWH's word delivered through his prophets."[229] In relating step by step the vengeance against the Ahabites, the narrator has Jehu himself voicing this theme of fulfillment three times. The first time is at Jezreel where Jehu meets the king Joram of Israel and his confederate, king Ahaziah of Judah. They have come to accost Jehu who, driving "like a maniac" from the battlefront, Jabesh Gilead, there kills king Joram. Jehu tells his aide to lift the dead king out of his chariot and to

> "throw him on the plot of ground belonging to Naboth the Jezreelite, for remember when you and I rode side by side behind his father Ahab how the Lord uttered this oracle against him: 'For the blood of Naboth and for the blood of his children that I saw yesterday, says Yahweh, I swear I will repay you on this very plot of ground.' Now therefore lift him out and throw him on the plot of ground in accordance with the word of Yahweh." (2 Kings 9:25-26)

Jehu voices this theme the second time at the death of Jezebel, also at Jezreel, at the king's palace. When two eunuchs look out of the palace window Jehu commands them to throw Jezebel down; they throw her down, "so that some of her blood splattered on the wall and on the horses, which trampled on her." When her burial party later reports to Jehu that when they come to pick up her corpse, the dogs had already eaten her, he replies, "This is *the word of Yahweh which he spoke by his servant Elijah the Tishbite,* 'In the territory of Jezreel the dogs shall eat the flesh of Jezebel; the corpse of Jezebel shall be like dung on the field in the territory of Jezreel, so that no one can say, 'this is Jezebel' " (1 Kings 9:36-37, emph. added).

The third time that Jehu voices the theme of Yahweh's fulfillment of the divine word is again at Jezreel, on this occasion after he had "killed all who were left of the house of Ahab in Jezreel, all his leaders, close friends, and priests, until he left him no survivor: Know then that *there shall fall to the earth nothing of the word of Yahweh, which Yahweh spoke concerning the house of Ahab; for Yahweh has done what he said through his servant Elijah*" (2 Kings 10:10-11, emph. added).

It is notable that Jehu makes this statement at the gate of Jezreel where, piled in two heaps are the heads of the sons of king Joram. He finds it necessary to justify his traitorous act before the people by appealing to this word of Yahweh through

Elijah: "You are innocent; it was I who conspired against my master and killed him. . . " (2 Kings 10:9).

Once more this theme of the fulfillment of Yahweh's word through the prophet Elijah is repeated in these two chapters, this time as a comment by the narrator. The occasion is when Jehu takes Jehonadab the son of Rechab[230] up into his chariot, saying: "Come with me and see my *zeal for Yahweh* (emph. added);" the narrator thus ties Jehu's action linguistically to that of Elijah (cf. 1 Kings 18:40; 19:10, 14). When they arrive at the capital city, Jehu kills "all that were left to Ahab in Samaria, until," as the narrator says, "he had wiped them out, *according to the word of Yahweh that he spoke to Elijah*" (2 Kings 10:17, emph. added).

The four repetitions of this theme—stated three times by Jehu and once by the narrator—could hardly make the point more emphatic: The canonical narrator affirms Jehu's use of Elijah's oracle to legitimize religiously and politically his bloody retribution against the Omri-Ahab dynasty.

But is that all he does? To understand the narrator's attitude more precisely, I will make a flashback of three royal generations, to revisit the scene of Elijah's indictment against king Ahab: "Have you killed and also taken possession" (1 Kings 21:19)?

NABOTH'S VINEYARD—A FLASHBACK, I KINGS 21

"Avenge the blood of Naboth!" This "clarion call of the revolt" re-echoes across the dynasty of Omri-Ahab (Ahaziah-Joram) until, as we have seen, it is taken up by Jehu.[231] The dominant criticism against this dynasty is that it has led Israel to desert the worship of Yahweh;[232] this worship of Yahweh is stated in the first and second commandment of the Decalogue and is foundational to the structure of covenant law and social justice in Israel.[233]

The central issue of the story of Naboth's vineyard is not one of "fairness"; Ahab offers him "a better vineyard for it," or, if that is not satisfactory, to give him "its value in money" (1 Kings 21:2).[234] But Naboth's objection is not merely an economic one; it is an objection to a theological-social change and its economic consequences—one might call Naboth's position "covenant economics:" *"Yahweh forbid* that I give you *my ancestral inheritance* (21:3, emph. added).

At issue are two religions with different systems of economics. Ahab's system involves a Baalistic property distribution based on kingship power. Naboth's system assumes a Yahwistic property distribution made in early Israel through its religious institutions to its tribes and families, and dependent thereafter on the people's commitment to this inalienable "ancestral inheritance" (Josh. 13–29; cf. Lev. 25; Ezek. 47:21-23).[235] King Ahab is proposing an "equal exchange" with *strings attached*; he is asking Naboth to surrender his economic independence under covenant with Yahweh! John Gray says of Naboth's rejection:

> To have accepted Ahab's proposal, fair as it seemed, would have prejudiced his own status and that of his family, relegating them to the status of royal dependants. In the administrative texts from the palace of Ras Shamra [an ancient tel in present Syria], we are familiar with grants of lands to certain classes and individuals at the king's discretion, usually with feudal or fiscal burdens.[236]

Naboth's position is not merely one of *laissez faire*—that government should interfere as little as possible in business affairs. It is far more radical: that economics should come under the authority of the fear of Yahweh, Israel's covenant God (cf. Isa. 5:8; Acts 4:32-37; 2 Cor. 8, esp. vv. 13-15).[237] For this covenant principle, Naboth died. Because of Ahab's deeply ingrained respect and perhaps even fear of Israelite covenant traditions (his children are given Yahwistic names), his kingly majesty went home and to bed, "resentful and sullen" at Naboth's refusal (1 Kings 21:4).[238]

Jezebel, from the Canaanite city of Sidon, is a Baal promoter and has no such scruples. It is evident that the law court is independent of the legitimate power of Israel's royalty, for to get what she wants it is necessary that she manipulate the assembly. She makes this a capital case. The charge is, "Naboth cursed God and the king" (1 Kings 21:13; cf. Exod. 22:28; Lev. 24:16). For other capital cases in the Bible, see that of Jeremiah (Jer. 26) and of Jesus (Mark 14:53-65; 15).[239]

Naboth is given the usual death sentence in ancient Israel, death by stoning (cf. John 8:1-11).[240]. Jezebel then says to Ahab, "Go take possession . . . ; for Naboth is . . . dead" (21:14). In the case of Jesus, the decision of the high priest, chief priests, elders, and scribes is, "All of them condemned him as deserving death" (Mark 14:64). Later Pilate "handed him over to be crucified" (15:15).

But there is another institution in ancient Israel, that of prophecy, that functions under Yahweh's direct commission when covenant justice is violated:

> Yahweh came to Elijah the Tishbite, saying, "Go down to meet king Ahab of Israel. . . . You shall say to him, 'Thus says Yahweh: Have you killed and also taken possession?' "You shall say to him, 'Thus says Yahweh: In the place where dogs licked up the blood of Naboth, dogs will also lick up your blood.'" (Lind trans., cf. 1 Kings 21:17-19)

In this commission, the prophet is first to announce Ahab's indictment; covenant justice is not arbitrary, but is based on law. The reason for judgment is that Ahab has broken the sixth and eighth commandments of the Decalogue.[241] This relationship of "the law and the prophet" must be recognized as a first principle for understanding respectively, both Israel's law and its prophecy.[242] For the editor-writer(s) of the Deuteronomistic History, the most important covenant laws are the first and second commandments of the Decalogue, the sole worship of the imageless Yahweh. This critique is expressed after Elijah meets Ahab, not only against this king, but also against his dynasty:

> Ahab said to Elijah, "Have you found me, O my enemy?" He answered, "I have found you. Because you have sold yourself to do what is evil in the sight of Yahweh, I will bring disaster on you; I will consume you, and will cut off from Ahab every male, bond or free, in Israel; and I will make your house *like the house of Jeroboam son of Nebat, and like the house of Baasha son of Ahijah*, because you have provoked me to anger and have caused Israel to sin? (1 Kings 21:20-22; cf. 14:7-11; 15:33-34; 16:12-14, emph. added)

It is the view of the deuteronomic historian that because of Solomon and Rehoboam's oppression, and worship of the nationalistic gods of Sidon, Moab, and the Ammonites, Yahweh through prophetic oracle breaks up the political kingdom ruled by the Davidic dynasty (1 Kings 11:27-39). Jeroboam, though promised an "enduring house like David" (1 Kings 11:38), forfeits this by committing fatal rebellion against Yahweh: he breaks Israel's most fundamental unity, the unity of the twelve tribes in their worship of Yahweh. By breaking this unity, Jeroboam makes of Yahweh a nationalistic god, like Baal, placing the power politics of kingship above covenant law and prophetic word. Yahweh responds by an oracle through the same prophet, announcing the end of Jeroboam's dynasty (1 Kings 14:6-11). Thereafter, all the dynasties of Israel are measured and judged by that of Jeroboam, including that of Jehu (1 Kings 15:33-34, 18-19; 25-26; 2 Kings 10:29).

But Ahab sins more than did Jeroboam; urged on by his wife Jezebel, he aggressively promotes the worship of the Canaanite god, Baal, alongside worship of Yahweh (1 Kings 21:25). Breaking the law of Yahweh's social ethics soon follows, and the editor-writer adds an anonymous oracle against Jezebel: "Also concerning Jezebel Yahweh said, 'The dogs shall eat Jezebel within the bounds of Jezreel.' Anyone belonging to Ahab who dies in the city the dogs shall eat; and anyone of his who dies in the open country the birds of the air shall eat" (1 Kings 21:23-24).

Yet there is forgiveness even for repentant Ahab, a forgiveness that changes his sentence, even if only partly (1 Kings 22:27-29). This dominant theme of the deuteronomistic historian, repentance and forgiveness, comes to the surface even in regard to this king who threatens the end of Yahwism in Israel.[243]

YAHWEH'S LIMITED AFFIRMATION
OF JEHU'S BLOOD BATH, 2 KINGS 10:18-36

We have seen that in the narrative of the violent revolt against king Joram, Jehu justifies his three violent acts against the Omri-Ahab dynasty as the fulfillment of Yahweh's word spoken by the prophet Elijah (2 Kings 9:25-26; 36-37; 10:10-11; 10:16-17).[244] Then, in a flashback to the narrative of Naboth's Vineyard we uncover the theological-political and economic meaning of that event for the covenant-landed people of Israel—why the echo of Jezreel reverberated across the dynasty of Omri-Ahab to that fateful day when wounded king Joram returned home to his city for healing. Now, at the end of a still greater massacre at the Baal temple in Samaria, the editor-writer(s) make their own evaluation of Jehu's reign, and insert within it an anonymous prophetic oracle which, they say, had been made to Jehu:

> "Thus Jehu wiped out Baal from Israel. But Jehu did not turn aside from the sins of Jeroboam son of Nebat, which he caused Israel to commit—the golden calves that were in Bethel and in Dan. *Yahweh said to Jehu, 'Because you have done well in carrying out what I consider right, and in accordance with all that was in my heart have dealt with the house of Ahab, your sons of the fourth generation shall sit on the throne of Israel.'* But Jehu was not careful to follow the law of Yahweh the God of Israel with all his heart; he did not turn from the sins of Jeroboam, which he caused Israel to commit (2 Kings 10:28-31 emph. added).[245]

One can understand why Jehu is quick to justify his acts by reference to the prophecy of Elijah; by this he gains license for further retribution, even from the people of Ahab's own city, Jezreel (2 Kings 10:8-11). Thus he, like Jeroboam before him, uses religion to further his political goals, securely establishing for himself and his dynasty the throne of Israel. Does reference to Elijah's prophecy necessarily exonerate him from retribution for "the blood of Jezreel?" Does the anonymous prophecy that rationalizes "Israel's longest surviving dynasty"[246] mean that Jehu is innocent before Yahweh (cf. 2 Kings 10:9-11)?

Yahweh's affirmation of Jehu's massacres has caused considerable discussion by commentators, especially since Yahweh later condemns these massacres as reported by the prophet Hosea: "And Yahweh said to him, Name him Jezreel; for in a little while I will punish the house of Jehu for the blood of Jezreel, and I will put an end to the kingdom of the house of Israel" (Hos.1:4). Andersen and Freedman maintain that the prophet Hosea does not later repudiate what prophet Elijah and his disciples affirm in the Deuteronomistic History.[247] Let us now examine this issue.

A casual reader of the deuteronomistic comment in 2 Kings may conclude that Yahweh gives unqualified approval to Jehu's massacres. But one who knows the tradition of limited retribution to the fourth generation, and the infinitude of blessing for those who love Yahweh as stated in the Decalogue (Exod. 20:5; Deut. 5:9) may on second thought be impressed by Yahweh's subtle limitation of blessing: "Your sons of the fourth generation shall sit on the throne of Israel" (cf. 1 Kings 11:38).[248]

Yahweh religion is not simplistic. The editor who reports Yahweh's approval of Jehu's blood bath also records divine limitation of blessing; because "Jehu was not careful to follow the law of Yahweh the God of Israel with all his heart; he did not turn from the sins of Jeroboam," who prioritized politics over religion by breaking the unity of Israel's worship for his own political advantage (2 Kings 10:31; cf. Exod. 20:7).

Four generations later (Jehu, Jehoahaz, Jehoash, Jeroboam II), the echo of *Jezreel* reverberates into the eighth century. The prophet Hosea announces that the time of limited blessing is nearly over, and the time of Jehu's retribution has come. Yahweh says to the prophet, "I will punish the house of Jehu for the blood of *Jezreel*" (Hos. 1:4, emph. added). It is time again for retribution, this time for Jehu who, though he had done "all that was in Yahweh's heart," had nevertheless by that act rejected the perfection of Yahweh. Hosea intimates that Jehu—in his act of violence—does not know Yahweh.[249] The dynasty will suffer divine punishment for the blood of Jezreel (Hos. 4:1-2; cf. Isa. 45:4-5 of Cyrus).[250]

At the end of the four generation period of limited blessing, the prophet Hosea discerns that new winds are blowing. Hosea 1–3 form the first segment of his book. As with the Moses and Elijah narratives that tell of their respective Sinai/Horeb experiences, this segment also has an envelope structure. Hosea's individual experience with Yahweh dominates chapters 1 and 3, while Israel's communal experience with Yahweh—the central point of the segment—dominates chapter 2 (Hebrew; Eng. 1:10-2:23).

Freedman and Andersen are right, I believe, in maintaining that the prophet Hosea does not repudiate what prophet

Elijah and his disciples affirm in the Deuteronomistic History. Hosea's understanding of the retribution due to the Jehu dynasty is no different from that of the anonymous prophet of the deuteronomic historian (2 Kings 10:30-31), who understands Yahweh's approbation of Jehu as only partial. The question of the deuteronomistic historian is why none of the Northern Kings are rewarded with an eternal dynasty as was David of Judah. (cf. 1 Kings 11:38).

> For the author of Kings . . . , the historical approach, the choice of events reported, the manner of presentation are governed by a single idea: the loyalty of the monarch to the God of Israel as worshipped in Jerusalem determines the course of history. In view of the catastrophic end of the northern kingdom and the pending doom foretold against Judah, the historian leveled severe criticism at the conduct of every monarch of Israel and most of those of Judah.[251]

HOSEA'S FAMILY EXPERIENCE
ILLUSTRATES ISRAEL'S BROKEN COVENANT, HOSEA 1:2-9

Hosea 1, a biography likely written by Hosea's disciple,[252] tells how Yahweh appears to Hosea four times over a period of several years. In Yahweh's first word to Hosea, the prophet is told to have a dysfunctional family: "Take for yourself a wife of whoredom and have children of whoredom." This astonishing demand is to illustrate to Hosea and Israel the dysfunctional relationship between Yahweh and the land: "for the land commits great whoredom by forsaking Yahweh" (Hos. 1:2; cf. 1 Kings 19:10, 14; Exod. 20:5 where different Hebrew vocabularies are used to express the same point).

Yahweh's second word to Hosea, the naming of his first son, connects with Jehu's blood bath: "Name him *Jezreel,* for in a little while I will punish the house of *Jehu* for *the blood of Jezreel,* and I will put an end to the kingdom of the house of Israel" (emph. added, Hos. 1:4; cf. 2 Kings 9:14-26; 30-37; 10:1-11). The name of Hosea's son is to signify to the Israelites not only Yahweh's retribution on Jehu's dynasty, but also an end to the kingdom of Israel: Yahweh will "break the bow of Israel in the valley of Jezreel."

Yahweh's third word to Hosea names the prophet's only daughter: "Name her *Lo-ruhamah* (Not Pitied) for I will no longer have pity on the house of Israel or forgive them." But it is different with the kingdom of Judah; here again, God will act as promised in Sinai's policy law, the Decalogue, "showing steadfast love to the thousandth generation of those who love me and keep my commandments" (Exod. 20:6; cf. 19:5). Salvation will happen in Judah according to the central concept of Yahweh war: "I will save them by Yahweh their God; I will not save them by *bow*, or by *sword*, or by *war*, or by *horses*, or by *horsemen* (Hos. 1:7; cf. Exod. 14:13-14, emph. added). The salvation will be despite and from all these, by Yahweh's word as spoken through the prophets.

Yahweh's fourth word to Hosea names his second son: "Name him *Lo-ammi* (Not My People), for you are not my people and I am not your God" (Hos. 1:8). The name of Hosea's first child signals Yahweh's future retribution for the blood bath of Jezreel. The name of his second child signals the withdrawal of Yahweh's compassion. The name of his third child signals that the actions of Israel have annulled the eternal covenant. For Hosea, retribution has to do not merely with external punishment, the end of one's existence, but with the end of personal covenant relationship, an end that Israel has initiated by rejection of Yahweh.

REVERSAL OF NAMES:
NOT RETRIBUTION AND DEATH BUT
FORGIVENESS AND LIFE, HOSEA 2 (HEBREW)

But can Israel annul Yahweh's eternal covenant? The second chapter of Hosea (Hebrew, 2:1-25; English, 1:10-2:23), the center of the envelope, begins and ends with the reversal and reinterpretation of the children's' names: *Jezreel*, God Sows; *Lo-Ruhamah*, Pitied; *Lo-ammi*, My People (1; 10-2:1; 2:21-23; cf. 1 Pet. 2:10), thus forming an envelope within an envelope: chapter 2 is about this reversal of names. Also, the status of the harlot wife is changed to one of freedom with her spouse: as a Baalist, she once called divinity *Baali* ("my lord," cf. 1 Peter 3:6, still the term used of the husband in modern Hebrew); now she is to call Yahweh, *ishi* ("my man," as is the practice in modern

German). Instead of destruction and repudiation as a people, harlot Israel will be given new dignity.

How is this reversal to happen? Somehow, Yahweh must win over Israel's will. The entire chapter is Yahweh's soliloquy on how this change might be effected.[253] This effort to effect change begins with the first paragraph of the chapter in our English Bibles, verses 1-5. The children's lives are at stake, they are exhorted, "*Plead* with your mother [Israel], *plead*." The word *plead (rib)* is often used as a technical term for a legal trial. But this is no legal trial. This pleading—not with the judge, but with the mother!—is entirely conversant with covenant law, which by the motive clause addresses the heart (Exod. 22:21; 23:9); it fits well the gentleness of the whisper, the silence of the law and the prophets.

The reason for pleading is the unfaithfulness of mother Israel: "she is not my wife; I am not her husband" (Hos. 2:2). The intent of the pleading is that mother Israel put away "her whoring," her adultery, her violation of covenant relationship with Yahweh by worshiping Baal gods (cf. Exod. 20:2-6). The life of mother Israel is at stake; the technique law of retribution for adultery demands that Yahweh "kill her" (Hos. 2:3; cf. Deut. 22:22), and have "no pity" on her children (2:4).

This first paragraph ends with mother Israel's confession: her action, going after her "lovers," is caused by her confused theological thinking: "I will go after my lovers; they give me my bread and my water, my wool . . . my flax, my oil . . . my drink" (2:5 [2:7, Heb.]).[254]

But pleading in itself is not sufficient. The three "therefores" of this soliloquy introduce three paragraphs that indicate the further procedures that Yahweh will take to achieve the goal of Israel's repentance, her change of character (Hos. 2:6, 9, 14). The first of these paragraphs presents disciplinary action: Yahweh will block Israel's paths to her lovers by "thornhedges" and "walls," so that she is not able to "overtake" or "find" her lovers (2:6-8).

Hopefully, this discipline plus the pleading might cause her to get her theology right and to repent: "I will go and return to my first husband, for it was better with me then than now." But remember that this is Yahweh's soliloquy, expressing divine hope; knowing God is not achieved by prophetic pleading and Yahweh's disciplinary action.

The second "therefore" introduces more stringent measures (Hos. 2:9-13). Perhaps it marks the change of the message of the eighth-century prophets: Instead of proclaiming this or that passing judgment, these prophets warn that "The end has come upon my people Israel" (Amos 8:2).

The paragraph includes seven first person pronouns of God's activity: Yahweh will "take back," "take away" gifts; expose Israel (in military defeat?), "put an end" to festivals, and so forth. This sketch ends by naming the essence of Israel's sin: Israel "went after her lovers, and *forgot me*, says Yahweh" (emph. added). Worship of the storm gods of the ancient Near East, whose kingship law undergirds their way of communal life, is to turn one's back upon Israel's personal covenant God and upon the covenant between Yahweh and people (Exod. 24:3-8).

But this soliloquy ends with a third "therefore." (Hos. 2:14-20). Though Israel forgets, a forgiving God cannot forget Israel. In this and following paragraphs, only the language of love is used. Yahweh entices Israel into the wilderness for a new beginning. There Yahweh will speak tenderly to her. Out of this relationship, Yahweh will again give gifts. And Israel will respond "as at the time when she came out of the land of Egypt." This time, beyond judgment, the relationship will be different. Yahweh will take Israel as a wife forever, "in righteousness and in justice, in steadfast love, and in mercy and faithfulness."

This third "therefore" defies human logic. It is divine logic. Specifically how Yahweh will accomplish this turnaround, Hosea does not say. But Hosea knows that to effect this change in relationship will not be easy, even for Yahweh. In his analogy of Israel as a wayward son, he exposes Yahweh's conflicting emotions:

> How can I give you up, Ephraim?....
>> My heart recoils within; my compassion grows warm
>> and tender.
> I will not execute my fierce anger;
> I will not again destroy Ephraim;

> For I am God and no mortal,
> the Holy One in your midst,
> and I will not come in wrath (Hos. 11:8-9).

God's grace is not cheap—at least not for God.

YAHWEH'S COVENANT FORGIVENESS: PARADIGM FOR HOSEA'S FAMILY RENEWAL, HOSEA 3

Hosea 3, written autobiographically, returns to the theme of chapter 1:2-9, the prophet's individual experience with Yahweh. With that chapter, it forms an envelope around 1:10-2:23 (Heb. 2:1-25), Israel's communal experience with Yahweh. This experience is symbolized by the reversal of names. By his own broken family experience, Hosea identifies with Yahweh's broken relationship with Israel (1:2-9; 2:1-14). Now, Yahweh's healing of that broken relation forms the paradigm for Hosea's renewed attempt at reconciliation with Gomer (2:15-23). Yahweh says, "Go love a woman who has a lover and is an adulteress, just as Yahweh loves the people of Israel, though they turn to other gods . . ." (3:1; cf. Exod. 20:2-3 NRSV; 22:21; 23:9).

It is not my intention here to deal with such legitimate questions as ancient Israel's inequalities in the marriage relationship (cf. Gen. 3 for a narrative of the Fall of the family, especially v. 16). My only point is that Israel's experience of God's love at the center (Hos. 2:14-23) motivates and models Hosea's attempt to change his family relationship: from retribution and punishment to forgiveness and rehabilitation. We saw this transforming effect of the Sinai motive-model clause upon law as applied to the alien: "You shall not oppress a resident alien; you know the heart of an alien, for you were aliens in the land of Egypt" (Exod. 23:9; cf. 20:2). Instead of death and retribution, the word is Nachfolge Jahweh, to imitate Yahweh's redemptive act for Israel.

Hosea bought Gomer back for what may have been the price of a slave.[255] If so, this surely must have prompted Israelite readers to remember their redemption from Egypt (cf. Hos. 2:15). The mixed payment—shekels, barley, and wine—may suggest that he gathers up all his resources to make this transaction. Grace is not cheap even on the human side, the side of Hosea, man of faith.

But grace is not cheap for Gomer either. Just as Yahweh lures Israel into the wilderness for a new bonding, so Hosea says to his wife, "You must remain as mine for many days, you shall not play the whore, you shall not have intercourse with a man, nor I with you" (Hos. 3:3; cf. 2:14). Grace has its own law, its torah. Out of the divine-human bonding with its conjoined interhuman bonding, authentic faith produces its work. This discipline is not arbitrary and punitive but rehabilitative, relevant to Gomer's (and Hosea's) attempt to rebuild their marriage on more than a mere physical relationship. After "many days," sexual intercourse will then consummate their bonded relationship.

But grace has its risks. After Hosea has spent all and done all, will bonding happen? Yahweh will somehow win Israel's heartfelt response, because "afterward the Israelites shall return and seek Yahweh their God. . . " (Hos. 3:5). But what about Gomer? The text leaves open whether Hosea succeeds. Hosea himself can only respond to the command of God in faith, believing that what Yahweh commands Yahweh will achieve. But how? Perhaps only by a profound emotional struggle; in the hearts of Gomer and Hosea—and perhaps even at the heart of the Creator of the universe, in the heart of Yahweh. Hosea shares this risk—and this agony—with his God:

> How can I give you up, Ephraim? How can I hand you
> over, O Israel?
> How can I make you like Admah? How can I treat you like
> Zeboiim?
> My heart recoils within me; my compassion grows warm
> and tender.
> I will not execute my fierce anger; I will not again destroy
> Ephraim;
> for I am God and no mortal, the Holy One in your
> midst,and I will not come in wrath. (Hos. 11:8-9)

The point here is that Yahweh's act of grace toward rebellious Israel has become the model for healing in a broken human relationship. A new law of grace is effective for Gomer. Retribution and death, still a characteristic of Sinai technique law (Exod. 20:22–23:19), is subverted by the intolerable tension of Yahweh's love and forgiveness, characteristic of Sinai covenant and policy law (19:4–20:6). After four generations, "wind, earthquake and fire," the asymmetrical opposite to "the whisper," is now over.

The remnant of 7000, the wholistic number of the Elijah story, is now become eschatologically the whole of Israel who does not bow the knee to Baal. This community is united to Yahweh by a divine saving act; that act is the foundation and paradigm for covenant law; and that law and paradigm, as we have observed, begins asymmetrically at Sinai. This represents a break-through in relationship to the death penalty—but it still must be systematized into a covenant code.

3

Selections on Covenant Law from the Writing Prophets

COVENANT LAW AND AMOS 1–2

The book of Amos is a collection made up mainly of that prophet's oracles, which date to the mid-eighth-century B.C.[256] Amos travels north from his home in Tekoa, south of Jerusalem, and speaks to the people of Israel. Although he is speaking immediately to the Northern Kingdom, his prophecies begin with Yahweh's roar from Zion and utterance from Jerusalem, which withers the pastures and the top of Carmel (Amos 1:2). The name *Carmel* means "garden," "vineyard" or "orchard," and like the modern phrase "fertile crescent" may designate the entire area, the seven nations and their center, Israel:[257]

Northeast: Aramean city-state of Damascus.

Southwest: Philistine coastal towns, Gaza, Ashkelon, Ashdod, and inland Ekron.

Northwest: Mediterranean emporium of Tyre.

Southeast: Edom, its region, Teman and capital, Bozrah. Ammonites, their capital, Rabbah. Moab, its fortified town, Kerioth.

South: Judah and Jerusalem, original capital of all Israel.

Center of these Nations: Israel, the Northern Kingdom.

Amos prophesies that seven of these nations will meet their end by *fire* sent from Yahweh. Though fire is the direct action of Yahweh, their punishment includes catastrophic military disasters;[258] the people and king of two nations will even be marched into exile (1:5, 15).

The six non-Yahwistic nations will meet their end because they violate what Amos must have considered Yahweh's international law forbidding inhumane acts of war:[259] Damascus for threshing "Gilead with threshing sledges of iron;" Gaza because it engaged in the slave trade, "carrying into exile entire communities," perhaps through Edom's southern seaport, Elath. Tyre is guilty of the same international crime, not remembering "the covenant of kinship" (an obscure statement); Edom, "because he pursued his brother (Judah?) with the sword and cast off all pity; he maintained his anger perpetually;" Ammon also commits international war crimes: "They . . . rip open pregnant women in Gilead to enlarge their territory." Moab's international crime is that "it burned to lime the bones of the king of Edom;" this charge is obscure but may mean "a violation of the sanctity of a tomb." [260]

While these six nations will be punished for rebellion against Yahweh because of their international war crimes, the two nations who worship Yahweh will be punished for religious-political rebellion and for domestic crimes. Judah rejects the entire "law of Yahweh" when "led astray by idolatry," the "lies after which their ancestors walked." By violating the first commandments of the Decalogue, it no longer acknowledges its Lead Partner in a covenant way of life.

Israel, the climax of this series, is indicted because the more powerful violate fellow covenant members in three areas the law especially protects. The first is economics: they "sell the righteous poor" into slavery and otherwise abuse the financially weak (Amos 2:6b-7a).

The second, whether it refers to incest or to a now obscure pagan cultic practice, is a violation of sex and family relations: "father and son go in to the same girl" (2:7b).

The third area of the indictment is against pagan worship, likely involving sacral sex: "They lay themselves down beside every altar;" their "luxury" is made possible by oppressive economics. Thus the three indictments are actually a unity as indicated by this climactic statement: Their economics, sex, and worship are condemned by the Holy.

The common introduction of the indictments indicates that all eight nations are held accountable to Yahweh: "For three transgressions (*pešca*) . . . and for four. . . . " The term *pesh'a* is used of treaty violations in which the vassal rebels against his suzerain. (Cf. 2 Kings 1:1; 3:5,7; 8:20, 22; cf. 1 Kings 12:19) It is essentially a covenant term, and in the framework of Israel's relations with God signifies the violation of the major terms of the covenant—that is, rebellion against God. In this context it is often referred to as the violation of general standards of international morality—universal laws of God—expressed in inhumane treatment of one nation by another. That offenses against Yahweh's law are involved is clear from the fact that punishment is to be meted out by the divine self. [261]

But how are these "offenses against Yahweh's law" to be understood? In my opinion, Andersen and Freedman are right in rejecting their basis as "general standards of international morality" or "universal laws of God." They make a convincing case that these offenses involve violations of King David's treaties with these nations.[262] Although David himself does not win these nations by peaceful negotiations (cf. Josh. 24;[263] like other ancient Near East kings and modern empires he pacifies them by military power; cf. 2 Sam. 8:2), the Zion-Davidic covenant itself emphasizes at its center a pacifism based on "trust in Yahweh.," often violated.[264]

I suggest that Amos's ultimate basis for accusing the eight nations of theopolitical rebellion *(peshā)* against Yahweh is *Yahweh's covenant law with Israel.* The two Yahwistic nations, Judah and Israel respectively, violate the fundamental law of exclusive worship and domestic ethical law. Meanwhile the six foreign nations commit international war crimes in their treatment of one another's people, thus rejecting Israel and Judah's divine appointment as exemplary leader. Both exemplary leaders and the nations violate Yahweh's leadership and are thus condemned.

Amos evidently understands Israel's covenant with Yahweh much the same way as does the writer-editor of Exodus 19:3-24:8: The law of Yahweh is within the structures of God's covenant with Israel, and the purpose of that law involves the *nations.*

"Then Moses went up to God; Yahweh called to him from the mountain, saying, "Thus you shall say to the house of Jacob, and tell the *Israelites: You have seen what I did to the Egyptians,* and how I bore you on eagles' wings and *brought you to myself.* Now therefore, *if you obey my voice and keep my covenant,* you shall be *my treasured possession out of all the peoples.* Indeed, the *whole earth is mine, but you shall be for me a priestly kingdom and a holy nation.* These are the words that you shall speak to the *Israelites"* (Exod. 19:3b-6, emph. added).

Three relevant principles are stated here: (1) Yahweh brings judgment on the Egyptians because they are internationally oppressive. They make slaves of the Israelites whom they rule over with rigor (cf. Exod. 1:13-14; Lev. 25:43, 46, 53, KJV). (2) Yahweh brings Israel to the divine self in a special covenant-law relationship. (3) The purpose of this special covenant-law relationship is not that Israel might be set aside merely as "a peculiar . . . people" (KJV), but that by obeying Yahweh's "voice" and keeping "covenant" law, Israel might be an exemplar to the nations. Yahweh will thus serve as Leader of the "whole earth," to Whom it belongs—an alternative to imperial leadership, such as that of the Egyptians upon whom God brings judgment—so that Egypt will acknowledge Yahweh (cf. Exod. 5:1-2; 7:1-5; Ezek. 39:21-29, emph. added).[265]

These three principles are congruent with the thought of Amos 1–2:1. The whole earth belongs to Yahweh; both non-Yahwistic and Yahwistic nations are in rebellion against divine covenant rule as is stated in each individual indictment.

The non-Yahwistic nations are in rebellion against Yahweh by their imperialistic ambition to rule over one another, thus challenging the covenant rule of Yahweh. In this rebellion they commit all kinds of heinous crimes against each other's peoples—which Israel as exemplar to the nations should have taught them not to do (cf. Amos 3:9; Isa. 2:2-5; cf. Micah 4:1-4, esp. v. 4).[266] Yahweh judges the nations, just as God judges Egypt at the Sea (Exod.15).[267]

The two Yahwistic nations are in rebellion against Yahweh by their disobedience to covenant law: first, to its foundation principle of loyalty by exclusive worship of this One cosmic

God, and second, to its concurrent principle of loyalty by doing justice in domestic relationships toward fellow covenant members. They thus fail as *exemplars to the nations*. Because Israel refuses to thus emulate Yahweh's saving action (Amos 2:9-12), Yahweh will climactically judge this covenant nation just as God judges the nations who do not follow their exemplar— perhaps made known to them by the example of a remnant and by prophetic preaching such as that of Amos (Amos 2:13-16, cf. 3:9).[268]

While before Yahweh the eight nations are thus all equally accountable, the two Yahwistic nations are in a climactic position because of their unique responsibility, their universal exemplary role. The crimes and punishment of Israel are especially emphasized because it is historically the leader of the two in relation to Yahweh;[269] and it is the nation to whom Amos directly speaks.

Unlike Hosea, the book of Amos consists mainly of judgment oracles. His series, addressed to international failure, is important to our inquiry since it reveals the unity of Yahweh's covenant law for Israel and the nations, a unity adequately explained by the Sinai covenant-law pericope itself: By obedience to covenant law, Israel as an exemplar to the nations is to provide an alternative leadership to that of empire. Amos is called to address foreign nations again, this time to gather them on "Mount Samaria" that they might witness Israel's failure in its international leadership (Amos 3:9). This failure and its redress we will now pursue in the book of Isaiah.

COVENANT LAW[270]
AND THE BOOK OF ISAIAH: FROM ISAIAH 1–39

Like an intergenerational novel,[271] the book of Isaiah consists of the oracles and experiences of three generations of prophets. The location of Isaiah the prophet is Jerusalem during Assyria's hegemony in the Near East (Isa. 1-39, eighth century B.C);[272] that of the second prophet is Babylon toward the end of that empire's rule (Isa. 40-55, sixth century B.C. ; that of the third prophet is again Jerusalem, during the Persian rule (Isa. 56-66, sixth or fifth century B.C.).[273] The three separate prophets, the last two disciples of Isaiah of Jerusalem, explain both the diversity of the book's style and vocabulary, and the unity of many of its themes.

Instead of being based on the Mosaic covenant and law, the message of the prophet Isaiah is founded on a Zion-David theology. The term *Zion* occurs in the first portion of the book twenty-nine times, while *David* occurs nine times (though not all represent Isaiah's work). Although one would hardly expect his Davidic kingship theology to provide a base to criticize the policy of his king, this is precisely what occurs; Isaiah seldom legitimates what his king does.

As Ben Ollenburger has shown by a study of the Zion poems, especially Psalms 46, 48, 76, Zion is central to Yahweh's promise to David. As Creator, Yahweh, not David, is the true king of Israel and of the nations. Isaiah emphasizes that it is solely Yahweh's prerogative to defend Jerusalem; the proper response of king and people when confronted by an enemy is to trust and wait upon God (Isa. 7:1-9:7; esp. 7:4, 9; 14:32). They are not to put their trust in armies nor rely on armaments. That is to be the decisive component in their theopolitical foreign policy (Isa. 31;1-3).

This theology of Yahweh's kingship is associated with the ark at Shiloh brought to Jerusalem by David. Isaiah's emphasis on trust, though based on a kingship theology, is not essentially different in its critique of violent power than is the statement of Moses to Israel at the Red Sea, as recorded in our present canon: "The Lord will fight for you, and you have only to keep still." (Exod. 14; 13-14).

As Ollenburger says, while the exodus theology is especially suited for oppressed South American Christians, the Zion-David theology is especially relevant to North American Christians so that though in a position of power they may not become oppressors.[274] Yahweh alone "exercises a monopoly on imperial power!"[275] And Yahweh is one who sets the prisoner free. As we saw above in our study of Hosea and Amos, Yahweh applies only those disciplines which are essential to the prisoner's rehabilitation. As we shall see, Isaiah applies this principle to domestic as well as to international policy. Any foreign policy which mistreats the foreigner is, from the prophetic point of view, an evil policy.

The main body of the book of Isaiah begins with a poem detailing Israel's failure to achieve its mandate as exemplar for the nations. Despite this, Yahweh's intention will be achieved, this time by the initiative of the nations (Isa. 2:1-5).[276]

> In days to come the mountain of Yahweh's house
> shall be established as the highest of the
>   mountains,
> and shall be raised above the hills;[277]
> all the nations shall stream to it.. . . .

The instrument to effect this new world order is "instruction [*tôrāh*], and the word of Yahweh from Jerusalem." Though we cannot say precisely what body of "instruction" and "word of Yahweh" the prophet envisions here, likely it is skills and traditions developed in settling disputes between the tribes and the two kingdoms, now adapted to arbitrate international disputes.[278]

The fact that they issue from temple rather than palace means that, like at Sinai, law and ethics are oriented toward Yahweh—divine worship only—an alternative vision from that of Near Eastern imperialistic empires. In this political activity, judging and arbitration are used to settle differences on the basis of justice and mutual reverence for Yahweh rather than on national self-interest and a doctrine of a balance of power and threat of war.

This portrayal of future amity of international government by word of Yahweh is contrasted in Isaiah 2:5–5:30[279] with the existing domestic anarchy of Israel. Isaiah exhorts Israel to take up *now* its vocation as Yahweh's international exemplar for tomorrow's world governments: to "walk in the instruction of Yahweh."[280] The word *full* (Hebrew, *malë*) occurs four times in 2:6-8, indicating the four areas in which Israel abandons the "way of Yahweh": (1) Silencing their prophets, they are "full of diviners and . . . soothsayers" upon whom they rely for their vision and future mandate (cf. Amos 2:12). (2) Since they are preoccupied with international commerce, their land is "filled with silver and gold" instead of justice and righteousness. (3) Relying on militarism and the sword instead of judicial decisions and arbitration, "their land is filled with horses . . . and chariots." (4) Finally, instead of loyalty to Yahweh, "their land is full of idols" and patriotic self-worship.

The result of Israel's abdication of its moral and spiritual leadership is that internationally the "people . . . and everyone is brought low" (2:9). "The haughty eyes of the people, and . . . everyone shall be humbled" (2:17). "On that day, people will throw away to the moles and the bats their idols of silver and gold which they made for themselves to worship" (2:20). Israel is urged, "turn away from mortals, . . . for what account are they?" (2:22) The last verse of Isaiah's "Song of the Vineyard" says it all:

> For the vineyard of Yahweh of hosts is the house of
>   Israel,
> and the people of Judah are his pleasant planting;
> He expected justice, but saw bloodshed;
> Righteousness [*sedaqah*], but heard a cry [*se'aqah*]! (Isa. 5:7)

Summing up Isaiah 2:1-5:30, this portion begins with a positive portrayal of Israel's relationship to the nations as their exemplar (2:2-5); it ends with a negative portrayal of that relationship, the exile (5:26-30). This polarity forms an envelope for the oracles between, oracles that indict Israel because it has defaulted as exemplar to the nations. However, amid these indictments and threats is a portrayal of hope. Zion-Jerusalem's survivors, after Yahweh's cleansing, are called holy. Yahweh will create for them "a shade by day . . . and a refuge . . . from the storm and rain," presumably metaphors of threatening nations (4:2-6). As the disciplined remnant keeps its eye on this future it will experience help for the polarity: Yahweh will expedite their calling as exemplar to the nations, and will save them from the nations.[281]

COVENANT LAW
AND THE BOOK OF ISAIAH: FROM ISAIAH 40–55

The work of a prophet of the exile, Isaiah 40–55, is perhaps the most creative of the three segments of the book of Isaiah in portraying covenant justice as based on Yahweh's love instead of retribution and death. He prophesies that the Creator of Israel who, as in the redemption from Egypt "makes a way in the sea, a path in the mighty waters," will make "a new thing, a way in the wilderness" to lead Israel back home from exile (Isa. 43:15-19). Retribution is over!

Relating to our subject, *the law and the prophets*, the climax of Isaiah 40–55 is found in the four traditional servant poems (42:1-6; 49:1-5; 50:4-9; 52:13-53:12).[282] Together the poems may form a biography of a public servant: the first poem presenting his installation into public life; the last reviews his end and reflects on the meaning of his public service.[283] I present five themes of these poems that relate to our topic:

(1) The servant is commissioned to establish Yahweh's *justice* in the nations (42:1–4).

(2) The servant is equipped with Yahweh's Spirit and is to effect Yahweh's justice *nonviolently*, by means of Yahweh's word (42:2-3; 49:2; 50:4-5).

(3) The servant encounters mounting opposition to his message of Yahweh's justice, opposition that apparently issues in his death. All this he patiently accepts in pursuit of his task (42:4; 49:4; 50:6-9; 52:13-53:12).

(4) The servant achieves his purpose to establish Yahweh's justice among the nations, but only by Yahweh's intervention; God reverses the nations' judgment against the servant by elevating him to a place of rule (52:13-15; 53:12).

(5) The kings and nations confess their rebellion against Yahweh and acknowledge that the suffering of the servant is on their behalf, that "by his bruises" they are healed (53:1-10).

The nonviolent ministry of this servant contrasts with the work of Cyrus who, though anointed as shepherd king by Yahweh to rebuild Jerusalem and return Israel to that city, does so by violence (Isa. 44:28-45:5; cf. 46:11). Though Yahweh calls Cyrus by his name and arms him for his work, the oracle emphasizes twice that "you do not know me" (Isa. 45:4-5).

Though Yahweh's messiah, this violent Cyrus never becomes Yahweh's "king of justice"; rather, Yahweh's justice for the nations is the task of the nonviolent prophet of the Servant Poems (Isa. 42:1-4; cf. ANET: 177b-178a). As in the Pentateuch all law codes are prophetic covenant codes rather than kingship codes, so this prophetic figure rather than the violent emperor Cyrus is servant of Yahweh's covenant law and justice to the nations. This covenant war God, Yahweh, establishes covenant justice in the nations by the "sheer silence" of a receptive, suffering prophet, unlike the "baalistic" war god of the emperor Cyrus, who speaks through wind and fire.

COVENANT LAW
AND THE BOOK OF EZEKIEL, EZEKIEL 18

Ezekiel revises covenant law in Babylon by limiting retribution to the first generation: "It is only the person who sins that shall die" (18:4; cf. Deut. 24:16;[284] Exod. 20:5). Even then, this wicked person will not die if he repents (18:21). One of the catalogues of sins for which a repentant person will not die includes the sin of murder: "a son who is violent, a shedder of blood" (18:10). Yahweh ends the chapter: "for I have no pleasure in the death of anyone. . . . Turn then, and live" (18:32; cf. 18:21-23).

Beyond the end, first threatened by Amos, Ezekiel promises resurrection (Ezek. 37: 1-14; cf. above, Amos). Motivated by divine integrity, "the name,"[285] God will gather Israel from the nations, return them to their own land, cleanse them from their rebellion, and put within them a new heart and spirit so that they will obey covenant law (Ezek. 36:26). Covenant love rather than retribution is Yahweh's last word (cf. Jer. 31:27-30).

COVENANT LAW AND INHUMANE
EMPIRES IN THE BOOK OF DANIEL (DAN. 6-7)

Apocalyptic writings appear among the Jews from 250 B.C. to 250 A.D. [286] The two complete apocalyptic books in the Bible are the Old Testament book Daniel,[287] and the New Testament book, The Revelation of John. The Greek word *apokalypsis* (revelation) is the first word of the New Testament book (Rev. 1:1); and the first sentence defines what it means: a revelation given by God through an angel to a seer, often to a people who are in distress, which tells in symbolic language what will soon come to pass.

The book of Daniel divides into two parts of six chapters each. The first six chapters are comprised of six narratives. The last six chapters begin with two visions followed by Daniel's prayer and an angel's prediction; then a conflict is reported between two empires, the Seleucid and Ptolemeic. The segment closes with an angel interpreting and instructing Daniel concerning the future, a future which includes a resurrection of the dead. Both the stories and the visions form an opposition literature of an oppressed people against the dominant Hellenistic culture of the times. I will discuss the book and covenant law by examining chapter 6, the last narrative, and chapter 7, the first vision. Together, story and vision form a fitting introduction to the world of the Sermon on the Mount and the New Testament.[288]

Two of the narratives in the book of Daniel are about capital punishment, a feature so dominant in both that the method of execution dominates their titles: "The Three Hebrews in the Fiery Furnace" (Dan. 3) and "Daniel in the Lions' Den" (Dan. 6). Were the titles chosen on the basis of their indictment, these narratives might be called "The Three Hebrews Worship Yahweh Only" (cf. Exod. 20:2) and "The Law of Daniel's God vs. The Law of the Medes and Persians" (cf. Dan. 6:5, 8). Both indictments have to do with worship, and even the structures of the chapters are much the same.

The issue of the story of Daniel in the Lions Den has to do with two kinds of law (Aramaic, *dat*). The law of the Medes and Persians is empire law, which is much like that of the law of Hammurabi, as this story illustrates. It is a political order established by warfare and enforced by police and threat of capital punishment. In this case the enforced act is one demanding worship of the king. A law of Hammurabi states, "If a judge gave a judgment, rendered a decision, deposited a sealed document, but later has altered his judgment, they shall prove that that judge altered the judgment which he gave and he shall pay twelve-fold the claim which holds in that case; further, they shall expel him in the assembly from the seat of judgment . . ." (# 5)[289]

The attempted execution of the three Hebrews (Dan. 3) is quite different from that of Daniel (Dan. 5). Though Babylon has its law, the king's edict demands the corporate loyalty act, the worship of its symbolic ideology, the golden image. When the secret police ferret out the non-cooperating Hebrews and accuse them to the king, they are given another chance to do obeisance to this power system—"and if not, who is the god who will deliver you out of my hands?"

The three men reply, "O Nebuchadnezzar, we have no need to present a defense to you in this matter. If our God whom we serve is able to deliver us from the furnace of blazing fire and out of your hand, let him deliver us. But if not, be it known to you, O king, that we will not serve your gods and we will not worship the golden statue that you have set up." Then Nebuchadnezzar, enraged and with distorted face, personally supervises their execution.

By contrast, King Darius moves to save Daniel from the conspirators of his own government and from his own law. "When the king heard the charge he was determined to *save* Daniel and until the sun went down he was determined to *rescue* him" (cf. 6:16, 19, emph. added). The Jews experienced that not all imperial systems were necessarily hostile to them. And when they were, their commitment to death freed the Jews from the empire's power. This is a different strategy of opposition to tyranny and death from that of the militant Macabbeans.

In contrast to the law of the Medes and Persians, the Jews possessed the law (*dat*) of Daniel's God. Instead of law within violent empire structures, it is law without territorial boundaries and, since the exile, taught within the covenant structures of synagogue worship and times of prayer. This prayer was never offered to the power structures of king and empire. Three times each day, Daniel comes "seeking mercy before his God." And through the ages it is from this God that covenant law communities receive deliverance from the oppressiveness of governments.

While Daniel 6 is a narrative about two different types of law, Daniel 7 is a vision about two different kinds of dominions or empires. The human kingdoms are depicted as arising from the sea in a chaotic windstorm as beasts, representing four successive world-wide powers, each different from the other. They are represented by a lion with eagles' wings (Babylon), a bear with three tusks (Media), a leopard with four wings and heads (Persia), and a fourth beast, nameless, with "great iron teeth, . . . devouring, . . . breaking in pieces, . . . stamping what was left with its feet," likely the Greek empire of Antiochus Epiphanies (Dan. 7:4-8).

These four empires, though differing from one another, have a common beastly nature. However, that one of them can nevertheless "stand on two feet like a human being; and a human mind was given to it" suggests that despite its beastly origin it can occasionally arise to the level of the human, though it may again descend to an irrational state (Dan. 4:28-32). The last evil beast is judged and put to death by the Ancient One; then Daniel "saw one like a human being ('son of man') coming with the clouds of heaven."[290]

Although in the Old Testament the phrase *son of man* is mainly used of humans in contrast to God, in Daniel 7 it is used in an exalted sense—some would identify this son of man with the angel Michael, while others with "the people of the holy ones of the Most High," in a corporate sense. (Dan. 7:27).[291]

In the New Testament, "the son of man" is used of Jesus both in the lowly and in the exalted sense (Luke 9:58; Mark 13:26). After the resurrection and ascension it is used of Jesus only in the exalted sense. The testimony of the New Testament Church is that God has intervened in Christ on behalf of the governance of humanity.

SUMMARY AND PROSPECT OF THE
TWO CHAPTERS ON ELIJAH AND THE PROPHETS

Elijah, traditionally greatest of the prophets, flees before Jezebel when she threatens his life because, after his victory on Mount Carmel, he has killed 450 Baal prophets. Disillusioned with Yahweh's lack of support, he journeys from Beersheba into the desert, wishing to die; but an angel diverts his flight into a pilgrimage to Sinai. There a theophany clarifies for zealous Elijah that his warrior God Yahweh, unlike the warrior god Baal, is identified not with storm and royal violence but with the "sound of sheer silence," with prophetic communication.

This "whisper" or "sheer silence," the forth element in the theophany, matches the fourth element in Elijah's commission: "Yet I will leave seven thousand in Israel . . ." (1 Kings 19:18). This community with the wholistic number of seven thousand is nurtured by the prophetic receptivity of Elisha, Elijah's successor, who made his rounds from Jericho to Gilgal, Bethel, and Carmel. As a disciple, his ministry is united with that of Elijah by the inclusio, "the chariots of Israel and its horsemen."

Elijah's positive clarification of Sinai, the prophetic receptivity or "sound of . . . silence" at the Center of Elijah's Horeb experience, is yet to work itself out, however, in its tension with Sinai technique law, law as applied at the city gate and elsewhere by local and royal power. There follows the blood bath of Jehu that is affirmed by Yahweh, but only partly; that is, for a time: to the "fourth generation" of Jehu's dynasty. Though this act is one of blessing; it is not a blessing to infinity, to the "thousandth generation" like that of the "enduring house" of David (1 Kings 11:38).

Yahweh's naming of Hosea's first son exposes the reason for the limits of Jehu's blessing, its tragic obverse side: "I will punish the house of Jehu for the blood of Jezreel. . . . I will break the bow of Israel in the valley of Jezreel" (Hos. 1:4-5). Even in a good cause, unleashed retribution bears with it certain penalties, in this case the penalty of death, death of a dynasty and of a nation.

While Hosea's tragic family life is symbolic of Israel's apostasy and sentence of death, Yahweh's redemption of Israel is the explicit paradigm for the redemption of Gomer. Hosea's action toward errant Gomer is not to be the retribution of divorce or death penalty; rather, he is to reestablish their marriage and by mutual disciplines is to heal their relationship. Hosea learns the incompatibility of technique law and its death penalty with the Sinai covenant's policy law of redemption and infinite forgiveness.

Though this is a giant leap in the development of covenant law and a fruition of Elijah's theophany on Mount Horeb, it has its early precedents in the model-motive clause attached to individual laws of the covenant law code, as this and other technique law is increasingly theologized and made congruent with basic covenant law (Exod. 19:4-6; 20:2; 22:21; 23:9; Deut. 15:12-8). The word is Nachfolge Jahweh—human imitation of Yahweh's divine acts of salvation for Israel and the world, a principle which does not contravene but is basic to Sinai law.

The prophets are closely involved with this covenant law, interpreting and applying it to new domestic and international situations. The first two chapters of the book of Amos are made up of a series of oracles that addresses international failure; it reveals the unity of Yahweh's covenant law for Israel and the nations, a unity adequately explained by the Sinai law pericope itself: By obedience to covenant law, Israel is to provide an alternative leadership to that of the Near East empires and to be an exemplar to the nations.

Isaiah of Jerusalem envisions the nations coming up to Zion to learn to walk in Yahweh's law (torah) and calls his own people to walk in this light. As an instrument for judging and arbitrating international disputes, covenant law makes war obsolete; biblical pacifism is here defined not as a "peace" achieved by retribution and violent pacification but as a peaceful strategy and firm intention to settle disputes between nations and peoples on the basis of Yahweh's law or instruction.

The book of Isaiah climaxes in the Servant Poems of the Babylonian prophet of the exile. In these poems a prophetic personality carries Yahweh's justice and forgiveness to the nations. The servant of these poems is contrasted with the Persian emperor by the Cyrus Poems: As Yahweh's messiah Cyrus returns the exiles to Jerusalem and rebuilds the city. But he does not know Israel's God and never becomes Yahweh's king of justice; justice is rather the role of the servant.

Finally, the prophet Ezekiel not only challenges retribution as a principle in the historical situation as did Hosea, but addresses the covenant law codes themselves with the radical assertion that even for murder the repentant sinner shall not die. At last, this noted corrector of technique law makes that law congruent with the principle of policy law, Nachfolge Jahweh.

In the apocalyptic book of Daniel,[292]this God of the suffering prophet teaches nonviolent resistance through the Wise Teachers (Dan. 11:32-35, 163 B.C.). Revealed in the New Testament passion narratives of the Gospel of Matthew (75 A.D.), this same God establishes the sacrificial suffering context for the fulfillment of covenant law as enunciated in the principles of the Lord's prayer and in the antitheses of the Sermon on the Mount.

4

On the Mountain with Jesus, Matthew 5–7

This is my Son, the Beloved; with him I am well pleased; listen to him!
—Matthew 17:5

LISTEN TO JESUS

On a mountain with his three disciples, a transfigured Jesus speaks with Moses and Elijah (Matt. 17:1-3). At the end of this appearance, a voice from a cloud says, "This is my Son, the Beloved; . . . listen to him." Having listened to Moses, Elijah and the prophets, let us now listen to covenant law as interpreted by this successor to the prophets, Jesus.[293]

The Sermon on the Mount is the first of five major discourses in the book of Matthew, discourses set within the narrative of God's gracious acts in Jesus for the salvation of humanity.[294] This may be compared with the relationship between grace and law in the Sinai text: First, Yahweh delivers Israel from the oppression of state slavery—divine grace. This deliverance then becomes the paradigm and motive clause for covenant law, designed to save Israel from oppressive relationships with one another (Exod. 20:2-6; 22:21-24; 23:9, 14).

Examined only linearly, the book of Matthew turns this order of grace and law around.[295] However, just as the Servant Poems in the book of Isaiah begin with the servant's call to establish God's justice in the nations (42:1-6), so this first discourse in the book of Matthew sets forth God's covenant justice. This is a justice for which Jesus afterward, as in the order of the Servant poems, gives his life for "the sins of many" (Isa.

53:13; cf. Matt. 20:28)[296]. Born to "save his people from their sins," i.e. from being rebels against God and from being oppressors like Pharaoh (Matt. 1:21), Jesus first sets forth the "higher righteousness" to which his disciples are called (Matt. 5-7). As first fruits of his passion and resurrection, his disciples are to be an exemplary community of light "set on a hill." After Jesus' ascension, they are to then go forth representing the Servant authority of Jesus. They are to "make disciples of all nations, baptizing them . . . and *teaching them to obey everything* which Jesus has commanded them (Matt. 28:18-20, emph. added).[297]

Read this way, the Sermon on the Mount, given first, is not a parenthesis in God's economy.[298] Rather, it is the climactic goal of the good news for the nations; the goal, set first, which Jesus' subsequent healings, passion, death, resurrection and gift of the Spirit are meant to achieve. This achievement is not only for the disciple community but through it for the community of the nations.

Viewed historically, the entire story of the earthly Jesus—the Sermon, his passion and resurrection—happens in the Old Testament age, before Pentecost. Written a generation after the death of Jesus, the gospel according to Mark (A.D. 69?)—used by Matthew for his own narrative (A.D. 75?)—sees the earthly ministry of Jesus in retrospect as "The beginning of the gospel of Jesus Christ, the Son of God" (Mark 1:1). Perhaps here Mark follows the practice of Near Eastern scribes: When the old king dies, the new king takes office immediately, though his official enthronement is deferred to the beginning of the new year. The scribes label this entire period, from taking office to enthronement, "In the beginning of the reign of [X]" (the new king) (Jer. 26:1; 27:1; 28:1)[299]

If Mark follows this practice, he then labels the entire ministry of Jesus, from his baptism by John to his ascension, "The beginning of the gospel of Jesus Christ. . . . " In any case, Jesus *is* the gospel, and this gospel begins with his baptism, amid the Old Age. The Gospel according to Matthew, using Mark's narrative, places the division of old and new between John the Baptist who "baptizes with water" and Jesus who "baptizes with the Holy Spirit and with fire" (Matt. 3:11; cf. Mark 1:8). So the new age, though future, is present *now* in the old, in the person of Jesus and his disciples as they minister among the nations by proclamation, precept, and example.

THE STRUCTURE OF THE SERMON ON THE MOUNT

The Sermon on the Mount has a "ring" structure with the Lord's Prayer at its center.[300] This may be compared with the simple envelope structures of the Sinai law code and the Elijah theophany on Mount Horeb.

The Ring Structure of the Sermon on the Mount (Luz: 212, revised):[301]

> 1. The Situation, 5:1-2
> 2. Introduction, Leading in, 5:3-16
> 3. Prologue of Main Section, 5:17-20
> 4. Main Section, Antitheses, 5:21-48
> 5. Main Section, Righteousness before God, 6:1-6
> 6. *Center: The Lord's Prayer, 6:7-15*
> 5'. Main Section, Righteousness before God, 6:16-18
> 4'. Main Section, Possessions, Judging, Prayer, 6:19-7:11
> 3'. Epilogue of Main Section, 7:12
> 2'. Conclusion, Leading out, 7:13-27
> 1'. The Reaction of Hearers, 7:28-8:1

The meaning of such a literary structure must be decided in each individual case. But the Lord's Prayer at the center of the "ring" likely indicates that the entire Sermon is to be interpreted in terms of this prayer.[302] Although one would not expect to find a prayer as a part of the law codes of the ancient Near East or of modern times, in this respect covenant law is different. The Sermon is like the Decalogue and Sinai covenant code in that it unites worship and ethics: "I am Yahweh your God, who brought you out of the land of Egypt, out of the house of slavery; you shall have no other gods before me" (i.e., in my worship, Exod. 20:2, 3; cf. 22:20; also, 20:22-26; 23:14-19). The principle, decisive for covenant law, is that one may worship only the God who gives freedom. This is the principle by which the remaining commandments are to be interpreted, including the technique laws of the covenant code. A command on how one should pray amid other imperatives about acts of piety, while quite different from anything in the Sinai covenant code, nevertheless shares that code's concern for the unity of worship and ethics, worship and law.

PETITIONS OF THE LORD'S PRAYER: FUNDAMENTAL PRINCIPLES OF THE SERMON, MATT. 6:9-13.

The Lord's Prayer consists of an address (Matt. 6:9b) followed by two series of three petitions. The address is made by a faith community to its Ruler: "Our Father." This family term for God occurs 17 times throughout the Sermon. This relationship with the Father is the context for each imperative of the Sermon. Covenant law is both given and enforced within the structure of this personal divine-human relationship. Some interpreters see the Aramaic term *Abba* as underlying the term *pater* (Father) in the Greek text.[303] If so, this may be a special term of endearment. The community itself consists of those who call upon their Father; it is not an ethnic community, but a community of faith.

Covenant law, unlike state law, is not limited by territorial boundaries but may be practiced by a faith community in any territorial state or empire—even if at times with persecutions. In the story of Israel's becoming Yahweh's people, covenant law is first given, not within the conventional boundaries of the Promised Land, but in the wilderness of Sinai.

Toward the other end of the biblical story, Ezekiel proclaims covenant law to the Israelites exiled in Babylon, a foreign land (Ezek. 18; cf. Ps. 137, esp. v. 4). In the Servant Songs of the book of Isaiah, the Servant establishes covenant law and justice among the nations (Isa. 42:1-4). And in the book of Matthew, the risen Lord commands that the Sermon be proclaimed to all nations (Matt. 28:20).

The first series of three petitions features the second person singular pronoun *your*; it deals with the larger concerns of God in the world (6:9c-10).[304] The second series of three features the first person plural pronoun, *us, our, we*; this series profiles important needs of the faith community (6:11-13). Of the petitions of the Lord's Prayer, I will discuss the four most relevant to the issue of the death penalty. These include the first three Yahweh concerns—your Name, kingdom and will—and one special need of the worshiping community, forgive us. [305]

The first concern of the Father that is pertinent to the death penalty has to do with the Father's name: "Hallowed be thy name." The name of God reveals the divine character, and was given to Moses at his call to lead Israel out of Egypt. The meaning of the name is not to be determined by some possible root meaning, though its debate might be of interest, but by association with the event at which it is given: salvation from state slavery. If believers maintain this ancient association here, then they are to pray that this name of the freeing, life-giving God is to be sanctified, set aside, and reverenced in the earth.

This is the first and all-encompassing principle of the Lord's Prayer: All ethics begin with God, with Yahweh's saving act for humanity. Believers begin their cooperation with God by orienting their entire lives toward the revelation and goal of this God, the one who sanctifies the divine Name. Like Abraham and the prophets of old, it is their task to petition God on the question of divine "justice" when confronted by such destruction as that of Sodom and Gomorrah.

By an oracle, the prophet Ezekiel speaks to this issue from the side of God: Yahweh promises to save Israel out of the nations to sanctify the holy Name. "I will sanctify my great name, which has been profaned among the nations and which you have profaned among them; and the nations shall know that I am Yahweh" (Ezek. 36:23).[306] His argument is that although Israel deserves death, God must save Israel because of the covenant promise to Abraham; otherwise the divine promise is broken in the eyes of the nations and for them the character of God is tarnished (cf. Ezek. 38:21-29).[307]

The third commandment of the Decalogue makes the case negatively: "You shall not make wrongful use of the name of Yahweh your God. . . . " While the idol is prohibited in Israel, the divine name is given so that God may be available to the worshiper. But this name may not be used for any purpose other than for what it is given, a saving purpose. If this interpretation is correct, perhaps Paul comes close to its meaning when he instructs how one should treat the persecutor; he says, "bless and curse not" (cf. Rom. 12; 14). Through the Prayer,

Christian worshipers desire the sanctification of the Name.

These first three petitions in regard to Yahweh's concerns in the world are closely related. Richard Gardner says that the divine act that will establish God's holiness is "spelled out in the second petition: 'Let your kingdom come. Manifest your reign in its fullness. Take control of life and history in every way.' When God's rule is fully established, then the request of the third petition will also be granted: The will of God will be done on earth as it is in heaven. God's will can refer either to God's purpose for history . . . or to God's will for our lives in an ethical sense."[308]

Unlimited by territorial boundaries, the "home" of covenant law is indicated by these second and third petitions: the Father's "kingdom and will." This kingdom or Rule is at the heart of the message of Jesus; the term occurs fifty-six times in the book of Matthew, ten times in the Sermon on the Mount. A future, anticipated Rule as in this prayer, with the person of Jesus it "draws near" in the present. In the first and eighth Beatitudes (Matt. 5:3, 10) the kingdom is present *now*: "for theirs *is* the kingdom (emph. added)." These two Beatitudes encompass the six others that are future oriented: . . . "for they *will be* comforted . . . (emph. added)."

Following such interpreters as Schweitzer and Chafer, it has become popular for some to so emphasize the future, apocalyptic character of the Sermon, that the present relevance of the Father's kingdom is denied.[309] This kingdom, however, is closely related to the work of the disciples, who petition both for its coming and that the will of God might be done here and now on the earthly scene—by direct divine action and by divine action especially through the disciples.[310] This will, its detailed features stated concretely by the imperatives in this Sermon, gives direction for the life of the faith community; it supercedes state law. It fundamentally opposes the state's self-serving character, although it may often support its detailed precept (cf. Matt. 5:10-11; Acts 5:29; Exod. 1:17).

"A city built on a hill," the exemplary community of disciples as blessed by God, is built there to indicate to the entire international social order its proper direction (Matt. 5:14). This universal kingdom, rather than the state or human community, provides the basic perspective for Christian ethics, including one's perspective on capital punishment.

The petition for forgiveness, the second petition having to do with human need, is perhaps the most demanding principle of the Sermon: "And forgive us our debts, as we also have forgiven our debtors" (Matt. 6:12). It is directly relevant to the issue of the death penalty. Forgiveness of debtors is not a precondition for God's forgiveness, as a casual reading of this prayer might suggest. The priority of God's grace is always presumed throughout the Bible, in both Testaments. Jesus and Matthew speak mainly to a Jewish audience who presuppose grace. Paul, however, apostle to the Gentiles, needs to make the priority of grace clear to his non-Hebrew reader.

Like Paul, Matthew clarifies this priority of grace in Jesus' "Parable of the Unforgiving Servant" (Matt. 18:23-35): "You wicked slave! I forgave you all that debt because you pleaded with me. Should you not have had mercy on your fellow slave, as I had mercy on you?" Jesus affirms the priority of Yahweh's Covenant love to human response, and therefore denounces as *wicked* the disciple who does not forgive others (cf. John 8:7).

The word *debts (opheilema)* as used generally, may refer both to "money debts," and then in a religious sense to one's sins or "trespasses" (cf. Matt. 6:14).[311] In the prayer as given in Luke 11:4, both words, "sins" and "indebted" are used, suggesting that, though the religious usage is primary, the social "jubilee" dimension of this petition should not be lost. In Levitical law, liberty is to be proclaimed on the day of atonement every forty-ninth or fiftieth year, and all Israelites are to return to their ancestral property debt-free (Lev. 25:8-55). In deuteronomic law, every seventh year debts are to be remitted for members of the community (Deut. 15:1-6).[312] As the apostle Paul explains it, the goal of the faith community is approximate economic equality, and this is a way toward achieving that goal.[313]

But as Jesus uses the word it also involves forgiveness for sins and obligations other than a money debt. Can even murder be forgiven? Here is an item from *The Goshen News*:[314]

SHOOTING VICTIM'S FAMILY
REACHES OUT TO ROBERT WISSMAN'S RELATIVES

When Wes and Mary Jo Oswald heard their son, Greg, had been killed in a Dec. 6 factory shooting in Goshen, their response was anything but expected. Instead of reacting with anger and hatred, the couple responded with love, reaching out to the family of the man who had fatally injured their son just days before.

On Dec. 12, Wes Oswald called the mother of Robert Wissman, who killed Greg Oswald and himself and injured several others at Nu-Wood Decorative Millwork Dec. 6, and told her he loved her and wished God's blessing on her.

"I grieved for her. I live with the death of a son. She lives with that as well," Oswald said. "My faith is strong enough and my foundation is strong enough that I'm not going to revert to (hatred)."

Carolyn Schrock-Shenk, associate professor of peace, justice and conflict studies at Wes and Mary Jo's alma mater, Goshen College, said such a reaction from grieving victims of a tragedy was inspiring, especially coming within a culture that emphasizes finding enemies and gaining vengeance.

"We, as a culture and as a nation, create an 'other' that we can oppose and make into our enemy. This is a family that has every reason to create an 'other,' to make an enemy because they have been so deeply hurt," Schrock-Shenk said. "They're refusing to do that.'

The Oswalds, of Lake Jackson, Texas, said the choice to give into anger and hate never crossed their minds. "My first thought (when I heard of Greg's death) was to pray for the family of Robert," Mary Jo Oswald said.

Wes Oswald added that he has a Christian calling to love his enemies, even in the face of a tragedy that would give every reason to hate. "The Peace foundation that I was brought up in, in the Mennonite Church, and that was fostered at Goshen College . . . that foundation is real. If you have built that foundation of peace and you sustain it over the years, it's there for you when you need it."

Shirleen Hoshstedler of Goshen, Wes Oswald's sister, said forgiveness (is) one of the fruits of the spirit. "For me, (our reaction) doesn't come from our strength," she said. "It comes from the strength of God." Strength the family believed was in Greg during the shooting.

Hochstedler said the family is not done reaching out. They hope to meet with Wissman's relatives to continue the healing process for both groups.

INTRODUCTION TO THE ANTITHESES: GREATER AND LESSER COVENANT LAWS, MATT. 5:17-20

The Antitheses of the Sermon apply as technique law what the Lord's Prayer presents as principles (Matt. 5:21-48): the petitions for the coming kingdom and present will of the Father, and for interhuman forgiveness (Matt. 6:10, 12). In the introduction to these Antitheses (5:17-20), Jesus begins by aligning himself in a positive way to "the law and the prophets."[315] Here he contradicts what some of his disciples have been thinking: "Think not that I have come to abolish the law or the prophets; I have not come to abolish but to fulfill." What Israel in the old covenant fails to do, Jesus in the new covenant will do (cf. Jer. 31:31-35).

Jesus speaks no word here about abolishing Near East or Roman Empire law, the law of human retribution based on the threat of kingship and the armed services. For Israel, "a priestly kingdom and holy nation" (Exod. 19:6), such law was abolished with Moses in the sense that it is drawn into tension and changed by covenant law. And that law which Moses proclaimed on Mount Sinai—covenant law, defended and nurtured by the prophets within the crucible of an aborted history—Jesus proclaims on the mount in Galilee that it is his intention to fulfill.

How? That we can know only through the account of Matthew. Like the Servant Poems, the story begins with Yahweh's justice (Matt. 5–7), and continues with the ministry, passion, resurrection, and elevation of the One who died "for many" to establish that justice. Now, with "all authority" he sends his followers out to disciple all nations, baptizing and teaching them all that he has commanded (Matt. 28:20; 5–7).

But what has Jesus commanded? Like a great rabbi, Jesus distinguishes between the greater and lesser covenant laws

(Matt. 22:36-40;19:18-19; cf. Exod. 20:1-17; 20:22–23:19). The lesser laws, like tithing "mint, dill, and cumin," are not to be so emphasized that in the minds of the people they become equal with, or even supercede, the "weightier matters of the law: justice and mercy and faith" (Matt. 23:23).

However, this does not mean for Jesus that one may become lax about smaller matters, since they, correctly interpreted, may apply the weightier principles to the individual case. The smaller, individual technique laws should be interpreted and practiced so as to *fulfill* the weighty principle, certainly not to violate it. For example: in this Sermon, Jesus favors laws of piety and is therefore very concerned about *how* they are practiced (6:1-18). Another example of his concern is how the Sabbath law is applied, a concern he discusses with the Pharisees (Matt. 12:1-14).

Moreover, prophetic interpreters of covenant law realize that significant social and cultural developments may demand changes in law to insure that life-giving justice is applied to each case as originally intended. For example Moses gives to Israel a "second law" when Israel moves from a nomadic to a settled existence (Deut.).

Again, Ezekiel simplifies and changes the law when Israel is exiled from life in the land to life in Babylon; following the lead of Yahweh's infinite forgiveness of Israel, Ezekiel extends forgiveness and abolition of the death penalty to the repentant murderer (Ezek. 18). Individual technique laws, laws practiced at the city or village gate, are also revised so as to "fulfill" the intent of covenant law—to give life and not death (cf. Ezek. 18). In another oracle Ezekiel reports that because of Israel's sinfulness Yahweh explains rather shockingly: "Moreover, I gave them statutes that were not good and ordinances by which they could not live. . ." (Ezek. 20:25).

Some commentators think that Matthew in the Sermon challenges the decision of the Jerusalem conference on the question of circumcision—like the Judaizers who challenge Paul long before Matthew wrote his Gospel (cf. Acts 15; Galatians). This is possible, as questions of individual case or technique law may generate disagreement, as in the contemporary instance of homosexuality.

But can one be sure that Matthew demands circumcision for Gentiles, since he mentions it nowhere in his book? Only Luke reports the story of the circumcision of baby Jesus (Luke 1:59). And in Matthew, Jesus sends forth his disciples to *baptize*, not to circumcise. Paul calls himself "the least of the apostles," not because of what he teaches, but because he has "persecuted the church of God" (cf. 1 Cor. 15:9). In any event, Matthew reports that Jesus does not excommunicate those who practice and teach freedom from a lesser law; they are indeed "called least in the kingdom of heaven"—but they do get in!

The repeated phrase "For . . . I tell you," Matt. 5:18 and 20, introduces the discussion on the "least" and greater commandments. As v. 18 introduces the neglect of the "least" which the Pharisees kept—which neglect still leaves one "in the kingdom"—so v. 20 introduces the neglect of the "righteousness" that "exceeds," which the Pharisees do not keep—but which neglect excludes one from "the kingdom" (cf. Matt. 23:23).

Jesus exposits these greater commandments in his six antitheses: "murder" (5:21-26), "adultery" (5:27-30), "divorce" (5:31-32), oaths (5:33-37), retaliation (5:38-42), and love for the enemy (5:43-47). We will discuss briefly the first, second, third, fifth and sixth antitheses, as these may be relevant to the issue of capital punishment. The fifth antithesis is the most relevant and therefore demands the longest discussion.

THE ANTITHESES AND
GREATER COVENANT LAWS, MATT. 5:21-47

The first antithesis concerns the sixth commandment of the Decalogue, taking of human life. Jesus speaks to the inner rage that incites to "murder," warning the disciple that the same judgment as for murder will be meted out for such rage. He gives notice against insulting a brother or sister with words that fuel the quarrel.[316] The polarity of murder is reconciliation: "be reconciled to your brother."

This impulse for reconciliation arises in a moment of corporate worship, "when you are offering your gift at the altar" (Matt. 5:23). Worship is a moment to "remember": to remember one's thwarted relationship, to remember this word of Jesus, his communal prayer (Matt. 6:12); and, from the later perspective of the community to which Matthew wrote, to remember the reconciling death of Jesus (Matt. 18:23-34). Then remembering, one is to act immediately upon what worship demands: to rid oneself of this incongruity between worship and life. In biblical faith, communal worship of Yahweh is the basis for ethics. Worship without reconciliation is hypocrisy.

Jesus contrasts this discipleship way of handling disputes to the worldly Greek-Roman court system, a system of "judge(s)," "guard(s)," and "prison(s)," leading not to reconciliation but to retribution. "Settle out of court," Jesus says, or "you will never get out until you have paid the last penny" (Matt. 5:25-26). Can the example of the Jesus' community change such courts? Certainly never entirely. Only by a constant example of the "congregational court," reconciliation based upon worship, can such a witness be effective. Only by participation in the "congregational court" can disciples maintain their awareness of the inadequacy of secular courts and therefore of the appropriate limits to their use.

One might contrast this teaching of Jesus with the action of Samuel at Gilgal, where he "hewed Agag in pieces before Yahweh"—i. e., in a worship service (1 Sam. 15:33). The long history of the incompatibility of such an execution with the intention of Yahweh's saving covenant relationship begun at Sinai— an intention fulfilled by Jesus as he insists on reconciliation at worship in the New Covenant—excludes such activity (cf. Ezek. 20:25-26).

The second and third antitheses—adultery and divorce— deal with the only social institution in the series, the inviolate character of the family within the theo-social institution of covenant. These are concerns of the seventh and tenth commandments of the Decalogue. And Jesus' solution may be directly related to the Nachfolge Jahweh as experienced by the prophet Hosea (1–3). As in the first antithesis, Jesus penetrates to the inner motive, this time to the look of "lust," adultery committed in the "heart" or mind (cf. Exod. 20:17). Here if anywhere in his antitheses, Matthew might appropriately have referred to circumcision, the sign of covenant, "the least of these commandments" (5:19; cf. Luke 2:21); but he represents Jesus as dealing only with the greater commandment, circumcision of the "heart" or mind. (cf. Jer. 4:4; 9:26; Ezek. 44:7, 9; Rom. 2:29).

Besides concern for the integrity of the married couple in their relation to creation, Jesus may have been concerned about the child whom, in Matthew 18, he blesses immediately after his discussion on divorce. Blessing, not curse and retribution, is the emphasis of the Sermon (Matt. 5:3-11; esp. v. 8). The inviolability of covenant marriage—as demonstrated by Hosea's rejection of retribution on the basis of God's redemption of rebellious Israel—is here affirmed by Jesus (cf. Hos. 1-3).

THE FIFTH ANTITHESIS: THE LAW OF RETALIATION

The fifth antithesis deals specifically with the law of retaliation, "An eye for an eye, and a tooth for a tooth." This statement is found once in each of the three major Pentateuchal law codes, in the technique segment of law (Exod. 21:23-24; Lev. 24:20; Deut. 19:21). The concept is also in the earlier Hammurabi Code;[317] in this code, as in modern insurance practice, a fixed money sum is substituted for the loss of a body member.

The biblical lex talionis limits redress of an injury to its "equivalent." Illustrating unlimited revenge, the Song of Lamech contrasts Cain's "seven-fold" revenge with Lamech's "seventy-sevenfold" vengeance (Gen. 4:24). Jesus turns this on its head by objecting to Peter's suggestion that forgiveness should be offered to a fellow church-member up to seven times: "Not seven times, but, I tell you, seventy-seven times" (Matt. 18:21-22). For Jesus, the solution to the problem of the broken human relationship is not retribution—not even the limitation of the lex talionis, equal damage—but forgiveness to infinity. This grace is not designed to undercut order but is the foundation of the New Order. Paul warns about presuming upon such grace (Rom. 6:1).

This protection of Cain from vengeance is later seen as the vocation of the Abraham people, as Abraham stands before Yahweh to turn aside *divine* wrath from Sodom (Gen. 18:23). Abraham's petition is not to be confused with an attitude of permissiveness—"anything goes." God is not permissive with Cain but demands of him certain disciplines (Gen. 4:14-16).

Humankind is created in the divine image; and all killing is an affront against God (Gen. 9:6).

The lex talionis (the law of retaliation or retribution) stated in Exodus and Deuteronomy begins with "life for life. . . . " But Hosea does not hesitate to reverse the law of retribution against harlotry and adultery, because retribution does not measure up to the central paradigm of God's love for Israel (Hos. 1–3). Also in the Sermon, the law of retaliation does not measure up to the word of the covenant God (Exod. 19:4; 20:2), nor to the measure of God's forgiveness as stated in the Decalogue (Exod. 20:5-6) and Lord 's Prayer (Matt. 6:12). The demand for retribution is native to Hammurabi or kingship law, but it is foreign to the motive-model clause of the OT covenant law codes. Jesus discards it for his disciples. As a "city built on a hill" they are by their example to project a new way of blessedness for the nations (Matt. 5:14; 5:3-12; cf. Exod. 19:4-6).

It is also appropriate to discuss here Paul's statement about being "subject to the governing authorities" (Rom. 13:1-7), since Paul describes the authorities as agents of retribution.[318] This text should be interpreted within the envelope of the two Scriptures that surround it, Scriptures that resemble the Sermon on the Mount more than any other of Paul's writings:

- Romans 12: 14-21, "Bless those who persecute you . . . ; Do not repay anyone evil for evil; . . . Never avenge yourselves; . . . If your enemies are hungry, feed them; if they are thirsty, give them something to drink . . . ; Do not be overcome by evil, but overcome evil with good."
- Romans 13:1-7, *For rulers are not a terror to good conduct, but to bad... . . . . If you do what is wrong, you should be afraid, for the authority does not bear the sword in vain! It is the servant of God to execute wrath on the wrong-doer* (emph. added).
- Romans 13:8-10, "The commandments, 'You shall not commit adultery; You shall not murder; You shall not steal; You shall not covet'; and any other commandment are summed up in this word, 'Love your neighbor as yourself.' . . . Therefore, love is the fulfilling of the law."

Paul is a realist. He likely would have agreed with Winston Churchill's statement as to how it is: "The Sermon on the

Mount is the last word in Christian ethics. . . . Still, it is not on these terms that ministers [i.e., statesman] assume their responsibilities of guiding states."[319] The Roman emperor at the time of Paul's writing of Romans is Nero, who later proclaims himself as divine, and is noted for persecuting Christians. Like Jesus in the Sermon on the Mount, Paul insists that Christians are not to resist evil with violence, but are to "be subject" to even this kind of "anti-Christ" authority: for "authorities that exist have been instituted by God" (13:1-2; cf. Jer. 27:6).

But Paul marches to a different drummer. Though subject to these authorities, he does not necessarily obey them. On his missionary travels he suffers "imprisonments, countless floggings, lashings, and beatings" from various governments who punish him for disturbing "the empire's pacification" by preaching and living the gospel of peace through Jesus Christ (2 Cor. 11:23-24; cf. Rom.10:15 KJV; Eph. 6:15). Paul does not hesitate to bring the law of the Roman Empire into tension with covenant law in those significant religious, social, and political contexts where they clash (cf. also Acts 16:16-40; 19:21-26).

The contrast between Paul's readers and the governing authorities can hardly be stated more forcefully. Which way then does Paul assume that the influence will flow? Who is "salt" and "light" to whom? The book of Romans is Paul's systematic statement of the gospel as "the power of God for salvation" (Rom. 1:16-17), and what this means for the vocation and life of the disciple in the church (12:1ff.).

In Romans 12:1, Paul exhorts the Roman Christians that they are not to let themselves be pressed into the world's mold. He envelops his description of the retributive justice of the governing authorities with exhortations from Jesus like those in the Sermon on the Mount, suggesting that gospel pressure, "the power of God for salvation," is placed on these authorities. Instead of disciples permitting their behavior to be pressed into the mold of the governing powers (Constantinianism), the disciples by living the Sermon on the Mount are to influence as "salt" and "light" the governing authorities of the Empire. The disciples are "not to be overcome by evil, but to overcome evil with good" (Rom. 12:21).

Jesus contrasts these two kinds of authorities:

"You know that among the nations those whom they recognize as their rulers lord it over them, and their great ones are tyrants over them. But it is not so among you; but whoever wishes to become great among you must be your servant, and whoever wishes to be first among you must be slave of all. For the Son of man came not to be served but to serve, and to give his life a ransom for many." (Mark 10:42)

This is the meaning of the Sermon in relation to the state: Because of the ransom of the Son of man, one can expect that, like the six stories of the book of Daniel, state authorities at least at times will acknowledge the authority of the God of Jesus (Dan. 1–6). For as Paul later wrote, "On that cross he [Christ] discarded the cosmic powers and authorities like a garment; he made a public spectacle of them and led them as captives in his triumphal procession" (Col. 2:15, NEB). The myth of the Machiavellian state is broken! After nearly two millennia of Christianity it is time for the church to proclaim that the right of the state to take human life is long since revoked.

It is from Matthew 5:39 that the term *nonresistance* comes: "Do not resist (*antistēnai*) evil" (KJV). As Jesus uses this phrase, it should not be equated with peacemaking, as this word is found in the seventh beatitude ("peacemakers," *eirēnopoios*, Matt. 5:9). *Peacemakers* is a more general term; nonresistance in this context is more specific, identifying how disciples are to react when someone abuses and persecutes them, as is likely when they are about their work as peacemakers. In this instance, disciples are not to demand their rights. Jesus gives four examples: a slap on the cheek, a legal suit; a demand to go one mile (probably to carry the equipment of a Roman soldier); a beggar's request. All are to be interpreted as examples of the disciples' response, illustrating behaviors opposite of the demand for retaliation and retribution (Matt. 5:39-42).

THE SIXTH ANTITHESIS: LOVE FOR THE ENEMY

The sixth antithesis is not the opposite of any statement in the Old Testament but is likely a popular interpretation. Here Jesus replaces hatred with love for the enemy. Although Old Testament law does not include love for the enemy (but cf.

Exod. 23:4), yet love for the non-citizen in Israel, the resident *alien*, is so important that it is stated twice in the exodus covenant code; and these two are the only interhuman laws in this code to which the exodus motive-model clause is attached (Exod. 22:21; 23:9). In the Levitical law, this alien is to be treated as a citizen: "You shall love the alien as yourself, for you were an alien in the land of Egypt" (Lev. 19:34).

This love even for the nonresident alien, the foreigner, is stretched to its limit in the book of Jonah, where the Decalogue's creedal statement of God's steadfast love is extended even to Nineveh, Israel's traditional national enemy (Jonah 4:2; cf. Exod. 20:6; 34:6-7).[320] As the prophet Jonah rejects this love as his own paradigm, so many Christians reject the model of the heavenly Father's impartial love: God sends "sunshine" and "rain" on both "righteous" and "unrighteous."

Does this paradigm refer to God's providence as experienced in the repeated acts of nature? Or is it a reversal of "Yahweh is a warrior," that is, instead of sending hailstones on the evildoer who attacks God's people (Josh. 10:11; Ezek. 38:22), Yahweh sends good things upon both the evil attacker and the righteous?[321] In either case, Jesus uses this statement of God's impartial love as model for his disciples. He rejects thereby the "law" of discrimination between neighbor and enemy (foreigner?) which some were evidently quoting in his day.[322]

PART TWO

RETROSPECT AND PROSPECT
Yahweh, Yahweh,
a God merciful and gracious
—Exodus 34: 6

5

From Law as Retribution to Law as Covenant Love

GOD'S LOVING ACTION IS THE TOUCHSTONE BY WHICH law is to be discerned, obeyed, or superseded. On this point Jesus and his disciples are consistent with the tradition of the law and the prophets (cf. Hos. 1–3; Isa. 40–55). In this way, Jesus weighs the practice of capital punishment (stoning), and finds it wanting (cf. John 8:2-11). Jesus said to the woman, "Neither do I condemn you. Go your way. . . . " However, while Jesus and Hosea are forgiving, neither is permissive. Hosea places himself and Gomer under appropriate discipline. Jesus commands the woman, "Do not sin again" (cf. Paul, Rom. 6:1).

Though he begins a new era of fulfillment, as indicated above Jesus still stands in the tradition of the law and the prophets. He is indeed the New Moses, with a final (eschatological) interpretation of covenant law. His law is founded upon a future act of God rather than a past act, a future act that becomes present in the disciple's walk with Jesus. The disciple has participated in the death and resurrection of Jesus, and absolute commitment to covenant law as principle is love's demand.

Yahweh's prophetic covenant is decisive to Sinai law. It is founded on God's act of deliverance from state slavery, an act which becomes paradigm and motive clause for both policy and technique law. In this code the ground of covenant law is a past act of God's grace, a law mediated not by a "king of justice" but by a prophet who communicates and actualizes Yahweh's covenant word in the present. Such acts may be defined in the Bible as those of the warrior God Yahweh (Exod. 15:3), or even of the Lamb's war (Rev. 6, esp. vv. 16-17).

Elijah's theophany at Horeb, which distinguishes between the warrior god(s) Baal and the Warrior God Yahweh, between law based on power politics and law based on the prophetic whisper or "sound of sheer silence," is decisive to a new understanding of Sinai and a new turn in the history of capital punishment. This whisper or "sound" in the prophet's experience displaces retribution by Yahweh's redemptive action as motive and paradigm for technique law, for healing Hosea's broken relationship to Gomer.

In the Servant Poems the prophet is called to establish Yahweh's law among the nations, not by war and violence, but by proclamation, and by taking upon himself the violence of the nations. This nonviolent Servant—rather than the emperor, Cyrus—is Yahweh's representative to establish justice in the nations. Cyrus represents Yahweh in returning Israel to its land, but he does not know Yahweh.

The Lord's Prayer is at the core of Jesus' Sermon on the Mount. The Prayer includes petitions for the Rule of the Father and for divine forgiveness even as disciples forgive others—petitions which the Antitheses concretize:

- by the law of reconciliation in worship in exchange for the law of murder and retribution in contemporary law courts;
- by the law of faithfulness from the heart in exchange for the lustful look, which leads to violation of the law against adultery;
- by the law of nonresistance in exchange for the law of retribution in technique law, and in legal practice;
- by love for the enemy, which has little precedent in Sinai law, but may be intimated in the Levitical law of love for the alien, especially as extended by the prophetic book of Jonah. This book might be seen not as an isolated fluke but as the ultimate demand of Israel's vocation as stated in Exodus 19:3-6, a vocation against which even the prophetic party rebelled.

Surely the saga from law as retribution to law as covenant love—begun decisively at Sinai and perfected finally on the Galilean Mountain—has been the narrative of a long journey. And it has been an even longer journey from that small band on the Galilean Mountain—a band sent out to disciple and teach all nations—to the *ecclesia* (church) of the third millennium A.D. The church polemicists of the first three centuries; monastic orders of the Middle Ages; the Waldensians and Wycliffites of the late Middle Ages; Felix Manz and Anabaptists; Menno Simons and Mennonites; Quakers of the early modern period; the early Wesleyans; the Catholics since the second Vatican Council; Catholics, Quakers, Mennonites, Wesleyans and others of the twenty-first century—all united against the death penalty, yet few are even aware of this journey!

The journey of Elijah to Sinai to distinguish between the Warrior God, Yahweh, and the warrior god, Baal—how many "disciples" have even begun this pilgrimage? Perhaps the dysfunction of the twenty-first century is not so much that of the state as it is of the church. We petition the Father, "Thy kingdom come, thy will be done, on earth. . . ." "And forgive us our debts, as we also have forgiven our debtors"!

Forgiveness is not the end, but a new beginning. The Sinai covenant code is given to Israel that it might be an exemplary community, leading the nations as "a kingdom of priests and a holy nation" (Exod. 19:5). Led by a Prophet from their holy community, Israel is called to proclaim Yahweh's justice to the nations. This Prophet accepts suffering as part of his vocation, and finally gives his life a ransom "for many."

Every prophetic book of collected oracles in the OT except Hosea includes in its oracles a message to the nations. The book of Isaiah envisions the conversion of the nations, that Yahweh's teaching and arbitration will replace war and retribution (Isa. 2:2-5); that the nations will acknowledge the vocation of Yahweh's servant (Isa. 40–55). Ezekiel presents by divine oracle that the nations, experiencing God's acts of judgment upon evil and seeing God's redemption for the covenant people, will acknowledge that: "I am Yahweh." Ezekiel leaves it open as to whether these nations become full disciples, or whether they simply acknowledge that the God of the covenant community is leader of world history (Ezek. 39:21-24), and come into some kind of relationship with that community and with its God.

Within the Sermon on the Mount and the book of Matthew this bifurcated vocation is presented: Jesus sends his disciples to baptize and discipline the nations, and the disciples are blessed to be salt to the earth and light to the world. How are they to do this? By accepting the eight blessings of Jesus; especially to identify, "in spirit," with the "poor," and to "rejoice" in whatever persecution may be theirs "for righteousness sake." The disciples are not to despair, because the future of the six Beatitudes is theirs (Matt. 5:4-9; cf. 5:3, 10)—blessing is not exhausted by Jesus' congratulations or wish for the disciple's happiness. To be "blessed" is to experience inner empowerment.

Hans Dieter Betz says that Paul would call the "specific attitudes, actions, and thoughts" of these blessed "'the fruit of the Spirit' rather than 'the works of the law.'"[323] By this empowerment, the disciple community is to challenge, qualify, and bring into tension the law of the old humanity, a humanity which still knows law only as power politics and retribution.

This book moves toward its ending with the statistics with which it began. The *New York Times Book Review* reports that although every other developed nation in the West has abandoned capital punishment, in America the death penalty is a booming business. It states that in just a decade "the execution rate has gone up 800 percent," that in 1999 more Americans were executed than in any year since 1952. Over 3500 prisoners—an all-time record—now await their destiny on death row.[324] Since most Americans claim a relationship to the church, there should be an interest in a discussion of what the Bible, especially Jesus, has to say about law and the death penalty. Or is American Christianity so tepid that such a discussion seems irrelevant?

6

Conversation with Law Professors Sarat and Shaffer

AUSTIN SARAT IS PROFESSOR OF JURISPRUDENCE and Political Science at Amherst College. Among other achievements, he has written *When the State Kills, Capital Punishment and the American Condition.*[325] Sister Helen Prejean says of his work,

> Of all the books that I have read on the death penalty, Sarat's probing analysis in these pages is among the best. I turned to some of Sarat's research when I wrote, *Dead Men Walking.* I trust his scholarship and his ability to construct a probing analysis of cultural assumptions and political and legal practice.[326]

My purpose in conversing with Austin Sarat's book is to connect the above biblical study to the present American situation.

THE CRITIQUE OF CAPITAL PUNISHMENT
MUST INCLUDE A CORPORATE DIMENSION

Sarat's main point is that in our criticism of capital punishment in America we must go beyond a personal moralistic approach, an approach characteristic of the present focus of most anti-capital punishment literature, to include a corporate critique. By making the argument mainly personal, Sarat says, Prejeans's film and others like it only endorse the status quo, leaving out the social causes, and so forth that cause the criminal behavior. Sarat asks,

What does the persistence of capital punishment mean for our law, politics, and culture? What impulses does state killing nurture in our responses to grievous wrongs? What demands does it place on our legal institutions? How is the death penalty represented in our culture? In addressing these questions, *When the State Kills* is animated by the belief that capital punishment has played, and continues to play a major, and dangerous, role in the modern economy of power. If we are to understand this role, our thinking about the death penalty has to go beyond treating it as simply a matter of moral argument and policy debate. We must examine the connections between capital punishment and certain fundamental issues facing our legal, political, and cultural systems. We must ask what the death penalty does *to* us, not just what it does *for* us.[327]

Austin Sarat examines these connections and fundamental issues in three parts. Part One treats "State Killing and the Politics of Vengeance" in two chapters: "The Return of Revenge: Hearing the Voice of the Victim in Capital Trials," and "Killing Me Softly: Capital Punishment and the Technologies for Taking Life."

Part Two, "State Killing in the Legal Process," he divides into three chapters, "Capital Trials and the Ordinary World of State Killing," "The Role of the Jury in the Killing State," and "Narrative Strategy and Death Penalty Advocacy: Attempting to save the condemned."

Part Three, "The Cultural Life of Capital Punishment," he discusses in two chapters, "To See or not to See; on Televising Executions" and "State Killing in Popular Culture"—the examination of three films, "Dead Man Walking," "Last Dance," and "The Green Mile." The concluding chapter deals with the New Abolitionism, which sums up and challenges us to address the societal issues as introduced in chapter one.[328]

Although Sarat may discount too much the criminal's personal freedom of will, the Bible presents a radical critique of state power, and especially of the state's tendency toward self-deification and violence. The Bible, much more radical yet than Sarat, actually gives an alternative structure to that of the state, a covenant law structure. This structure is founded upon

covenanted love and upon severely restricted violence as Yahweh's prerogative (Exod. 19–24), and ultimately upon the
words, death, and the resurrection leadership of Yahweh's Servant (The New Testament).

Referring to Robert Cover,[329] Sarat borrows from this more
radical biblical critique:

> For death penalty lawyers, "redemption takes place within
> an eschatological schema that postulates: (1) the unre-
> deemed character of reality as we know it, (2) the funda-
> mentally different reality that should take its place, and (3)
> the replacement of one with the other." Cover uses the ex-
> ample of an abolitionist struggle of another era, namely an-
> tislavery activism in the mid-nineteenth century, to suggest
> that the work of "redemptive constitutionalism" reveals "a
> creative pulse that proliferates principle and precept, com-
> mentary and justification, even in the face of a state legal
> order less likely to hold slavery unconstitutional than to
> declare the imminent kingship of Jesus Christ on earth." In
> this view, the lawyer serving a losing cause speaks in a
> prophetic voice even as she supplies the argumentative
> and interpretive resources to bridge the gap between the
> violence of the present and the beckoning possibility of jus-
> tice.[330]

While it is legitimate to borrow from radical covenant wisdom for work in the state legal system as Sarat does here, I suggest that to maintain its more radical vision, one must accept
the covenant law structures of synagogue and church along-
side the structures of the state as part of the governance of society. Indeed, from the biblical point of view this covenant structure is not only along-side the state but, on another level, up-
holds the entire society within its relational edifice (Gen. 9).
Furthermore it challenges the sovereignty of the state: "But the
midwives feared God; they did not do as the king of Egypt
commanded them, but they let the boys live."

Unfortunately, in our relation to capital punishment in the
United States, we do not have the control that the midwives
had in respect to the Israelite children. That is precisely our
problem, how to find ways to persuade. But perhaps even the
secularists among us can respect the resource of a community

whose leaders—after more than a millennium, and a turbulent one at that—can still speak in solidarity with the midwives on the question of authority: "We must obey God rather than any human authority." And they dare to stand their ground under threat of execution by a power-oriented justice system—though saved by an alternative logic of one of their own Israelite tradition, a Pharisee called Gamaliel who advised, instead of execution, to leave the case with God (Acts 5:27-42, esp. v. 29).

Is it coincidence that the people who led the early modern anti-capital-punishment campaign in the sixteenth century A.D. were saints, people whose lives were threatened because of their righteous faith? And can we trust a state that kills a criminal not to also kill the person who because of righteous faith may disobey some of its laws? The continuity of those who die, from criminal to saint, has an ancient history, whose vestigial roots are still evident in the Pentateuchal law codes.

Might a fitting symbol for those who assent to covenant law be not one cross, but three? One cross is antiseptically religious; three crosses involve the Holy with the lawless: "And he was counted among the lawless" (Mark 15:28, NRSV margin). The symbol of the depth of humanity's sin is the state's involvement of the holy with the lawless—not one cross but three.

Three crosses happen also to portray the historical Jesus. Paul, himself not immune to a death legitimated by the state, conjures up this threefold image of the historical death of Jesus:

> And when you were dead in the trespasses and the uncircumcision of your flesh, God made you alive together with him, when he forgave us all our trespasses, erasing the record that stood against us with its legal demands. He set this aside, nailing it to the cross. He disarmed the rulers and authorities and made a public example of them, triumphing over them in it.

At the risk of being tarnished by self-righteousness, I ask the question every United States citizen needs to face: Is the United States justice system so evil that it cannot allow covenant righteous people to participate in it in a positive way? Why must the righteous be excluded "by [their] faith" from jury duty in a murder trial (cf. Heb. 11)? Are "the righteous" at fault? Or is their exclusion by "the unrighteous" wrong?

What is to save this system from becoming the gulag some are already calling it? How can the world's lone superpower not worship its own projected image to become the Superpower? Only as it finds ways to surrender and share its sovereignty, to confess that there is a Righteousness greater than itself, and that its own might—even its majority vote—does not make Right. How does America provide for the honest participation of its moral minority, a minority with more than three millennia of law tradition? Or is this minority as dangerous to America as its criminals?

On the side of this minority there is another relevant tradition, the tradition to die for covenant justice. This means first of all, the courage to die for its covenant law and institutional structures that I have tried to explicate in this book. To die for covenant justice has meant historically to die not in a defensive but in an offensive mode. Are there legitimate ways the "suffering righteous" can speak to gospel-relevant public issues? Is the "deception" of the midwives or of the resurrected Jesus never warranted (Exod.1:18-19; Luke 24:15-29)? If so, when and how? How can church and synagogue move through locked doors?

Stephen L. Carter in *The Culture of Disbelief* says, "Simply put, the metaphorical separation of church and state originated in an effort to protect religion from the state, not the state from religion."[331] It protects not merely the individual conscience "but the preservation of the power of religions as independent power bases to resist the state."[332] Carter points out that when religion has done great evil it has generally been when it is allied with the state. The proper vocation of the covenant people is to acknowledge its own covenant law, and by obedience and proclamation, to draw the law of the state into tension with it.

THE JURISPRUDENCE OF JOHN HOWARD YODER AND SIXTEENTH-CENTURY RADICAL REFORMERS

I close this discussion by referring to "conversations on law, ethics, and the church" between a Hoosier lawyer, Thomas L. Shaffer, and a Mennonite theologian, John Howard Yoder.[333]

Shaffer sees in Yoder's work "an implicit theology of law, a jurisprudence and legal ethic."[334]

To gain a perspective on the church's relation to the state and its law, I refer to three emphases of Yoder's Anabaptist-Mennonite theology. The first is baptism on confession of one's faith.[335] This adult baptism, stated in an early Anabaptist confession,[336] separates the church from the larger society of the state, and in so doing has echoes of Israel's covenant vocation as stated in Exodus 19:4-6. In the sixteenth century A.D. this presented a radical break with medieval European society's emphasis on infant baptism and the unity of the church with the state. It is within the context of fellow-believers and covenant body of Christ's church that baptized believers find their identity for mission to the world.[337]

Another emphasis of John Howard Yoder is that he was above all a pacifist. Quoting Stanley Hauerwas, Shaffer affirms that Yoder turned around pacifism's loss of credibility due to the influence of Reinhold Niebuhr and World War II.[338] This rejection of the sword is also stated in the sixteenth-century Reformation document, the earliest such statement of any church creed: "The sword is an ordering of God outside the perfection of Christ."[339] This rejection includes the rejection of a magistracy which commands the use of the sword.

Since it is widely recognized that American law rests on legal force, the question is "how a pacifist practices law in the shadow of that legal force."[340] Yoder shows some ambiguity here. On the one hand, he makes the point with an inquiring young law student, "Well, maybe a Christian cannot be a lawyer,"[341] and wrote in his book, *For the Nations*, "It may be all right sometimes to acknowledge that there is nothing we can do to fix the world."[342] On the other hand, he cites political examples such as William Penn, William Lloyd Garrison, and Alexander Campbell, "sectarians" who had a "concern for healthy political life...."[343]

May it be possible for a lawyer in a courtroom to defend a prisoner from a death sentence in an exemplary pacifistic way? Can Christians establish an alternative courtroom tradition? The apostle Paul considers it shocking that a congregation does not have its own alternative Christian court (1 Cor. 6:1-8).

John Howard Yoder's position on pacifism and peace, however, is a positive one not defined by its critique of the state but by Jesus and his new community, whose initiatory rite of baptism is correlated with the repeated rite of communion, the opposite of murder and war. According to the synoptic gospels, this rite is established by Jesus at the Passover meal, which celebrates freedom from oppressive state slavery, and which, as established by Jesus, celebrates freedom from sin, one's violation of the peace of God and of fellow humankind.

Freedom from Pharaoh's oppression includes freedom from being like Pharaoh the oppressor. Yoder's emphasis is that it is only by participation in the *pax* of this new community that one can find a platform of grace from which to fight the good fight of reconciliation in the courtrooms of America. With the promise of Spirit, this gospel platform provides holy power and prophetic insight of where, when and how to attack the evils of society and state, and where, when, and how to withdraw into the wilderness "to rest awhile."

Yoder's emphasis of the church's prophetic relation to the state is shaped largely by Jeremiah's letter to the exiles in Babylon: "But seek the welfare of the city where I have sent you into exile, and pray to Yahweh on its behalf, for in its welfare you will find your welfare" (Jer. 29:7). This counsel was given to counter the advice of false prophets among the exiles who were prodding the exiles toward a violent solution to Babylon's violation of their human rights: "Do not let the prophets and the diviners who are among you deceive you, and do not listen to the dreams that they dream, for it is a lie that they are prophesying to you in my name; I did not send them, says Yahweh."

Yoder held that this is not a counsel of convenience to help the people survive the exile. Rather, it is a policy the Jews follow more or less until the revolt of the Maccabees. Then it guides the Jews again after the debacle led by Bar Kokhba, until 1947 and the founding of the modern state of Israel.

It is fitting to close this comment on Austin Sarat's work with the observation that while John Howard Yoder and the radical reformation reject the violent base of the law of imperialistic America, as Thomas L. Shaffer notes, Yoder draws our attention to an implicit alternative "theology of law, a jurisprudence and legal ethic" for the American citizen and lawyer. It is none other than the theology and jurisprudence of covenant law, a law which is won at no small cost.

This law begins with the theophany of Yahweh at Sinai, where the legal decisions of the Israelite confederacy are brought before Yahweh, placed within the constitution of Covenant, upon the foundation of salvation history and Yahweh's forgiveness The law is clarified and prophetically reoriented by the theophany at Horeb, which is the highlight of the Deuteronomistic History in its portrayal of the prophetic conflict with Baal and the creation of the community of 7000, begotten and formed within a hostile environment—not by wind and fire but by the sound of sheer silence. Finally the law is deepened and universalized by the eschatological moment of theophany at Galilee, founded and oriented by the three crosses at Golgotha, and fruited at the ecumenical gathering at the temple in Jerusalem.

This covenant law has survived the wind and fire of two tumultuous millennia to point the way and revive the spirit of the wounded community and global world of our twenty-first century. This law is *the sound of sheer silence.*

Notes

Abbreviations in Notes
ABD   Anchor Bible Dictionary
ANET Ancient Near Eastern Texts

1. My first real introduction to an American patriotism which justified the country's violent policy toward the Native American peoples and lauded American wars was in a little one-room schoolhouse in the middle of our Oregon Mennonite community.

2. Millard C. Lind, *Yahweh is a Warrior, The Theology of Warfare in Ancient Israel* (Scottdale, Pa: Herald Press, 1980). When my Associated Mennonite Biblical Seminary colleagues, Jacob Enz and others, encouraged me to write that book, I first wrote to David Noel Freedman for his counsel before I proceeded to do this; he gave me extensive suggestions throughout the writing of the book, at times toning me down.

3. Ben Ollenberger, *Zion, City of the Great King: A Theological Symbol of the Jerusalem Cult* (Sheffield: JSOT Press, 1987).

4. Christopher D. Marshall, *Beyond Retribution, A New Testament Vision for Justice, Crime, and Punishment* (Grand Rapids: Eerdmans, 2001).

5. On August 28, 2001, the PBS network published comments by specialists on the U.S. government's report as to the present state of American prisons. In proportion to its population, the United States now has more citizens incarcerated in federal, state, and local prisons than has any other nation in the world, including Russia. As long as this continues how can America claim to be "the home of the free?" One Bible scholar estimates that the ancient Israelite "slave" as represented in the biblical law codes probably had it better than does the average American prisoner. The nadir of this prison system is the extended death row of many of the American states, the state of Texas leading the way.

6. *New York Times Book Review* (Dec. 10, 2000), 34

7. Austin Sarat, *When the State Kills: Capital Punishment and the American Condition* (Princeton, N.J.: Princeton University Press, 2001), 12

145

8. Gerhard von Rad, "Justice, Human and Divine in the Old Testament," in *The Biblical Doctrine of Justice,* WCC Study Department, Study Conference at Treysa, Germany, Aug. 2-7, 1950.

9. For a definition of law and justice within covenant, see chapter 1.

10. Since this is the book's introduction in which I give a preview of the argument that is coming, I keep definitions to a minimum here. By "prophetic covenant," I distinguish the covenant of Moses from such statements as the prologue to the Law of Hammurabi and other kingship law codes, which some scholars have called "kingship covenants." For further discussion, see chapter 1.

11. Millard C. Lind, "Reflections on Biblical Hermeneutics" in Willard M. Swartley, *Essays on Biblical Interpretation, Anabaptist-Mennonite Perspectives, 1984* (Elkhart, Ind.: Institute of Mennonite Studies), 151-164; Willard M. Swartley, *Slavery, Sabbath, War and Women: Case Issues in Biblical Interpretations* (Scottdale, Pa.: Herald Press, 1983), 96-149

12. For a discussion of this scripture, see Raymond E. Brown, *The Gospel According to John (i-xii)* (Garden City, N.J.: Doubleday & Company, Inc., 1966), 335-338. Although Brown counsels against using this one story as a general norm against capital punishment, I would hold that it is decisive if added to other considerations pointing in this direction. And no one that I know advocates that the state kill those citizens who commit adultery.

13. For a discussion of the relation of this legal advice of Jethro to Moses in history and in the Bible, and of the civil structure and baffling military nature of its hierarchical system, see Waldemar Janzen, *Exodus,* Believers Church Bible Commentary (Scottdale, Pa.: Herald Press, 2000), 228-30.

14. Cf. Exod. 20:2-17; 20:22–23:33; Lev. 16–26); Deut. 12–26; 28; 27:11-26; *ANET (Ancient Near Eastern Texts,* ed. Pritchard):159-198, esp. the epilogue to Hammurabi's law (*ANET* [1] p. 177, [70] p. 178).

15. Hosea 12:13. May there have been an ancient legal practice in which prophetic-priestly successors to Moses continue what is suggested in Exod. 18? Cf. Matt. 23:2.

16. Although these ancient Near East "law codes" were not used as a canonical law to determine individual cases, and are thus better considered as "law collections," I nevertheless follow the common scholarly practice by referring to them as "law codes."

17. Harold J. Berman maintains that modern western law began in the eleventh and twelfth centuries A.D. under church guidance, motivated by a struggle for supremacy between pope and emperor—Berman, *Law and Revolution: The Formation of the Western Legal Tradition* (Cambridge, Mass.: Harvard University Press, 1983). Unfortunately, because of the Medieval unity of church and state, both systems of law were undergirded with violence. See my article, "The Theology of Law," in *Mennonite Encyclopedia,* vol. 5, ed. Cornelius J. Dyck and Den-

nis D. Martin (Scottdale, Pa.: Mennonite Publishing House, 1990), 511-12.

18. See discussion of Exodus 18 above.

19. The usual term for this use of the Egyptian and other clauses of God's redemptive acts and characteristics is "motive clause." However, this term overlooks the equally important use of such divine acts as model clauses—see Nachfolge Jahweh discussed above and below in relation to Jesus and the Sermon. Model and motive functions of the clause are equally important. See discussion in chapter 1.

20. See the discussion of Hans Dieter Betz on how the individual laws of the Torah are meant to serve justice. Betz, *The Sermon on the Mount*. Hermeneia Commentary (Minneapolis: Fortress Press, 1995), 178-179.

21. Clarence Bauman, *The Sermon on the Mount: The Modern Quest for its Meaning* (Macon, Ga.: Mercer University Press, 1985), 384.

22. For a discussion of Yahweh's vengeance, which Paul reminds his readers that Israel is not to imitate (Rom. 12:19), see George E. Mendenhall, "The 'Vengeance' of Yahweh," *The Tenth Generation*, (Baltimore: The Johns Hopkins University Press, 1973), 69-104; Mendenhall's thesis is that Yahweh's "vengeance" (*naqam*) is not to be related to the individual but to the public sphere. Already in pre-biblical times, "the root *nqm* signifies the executive exercise of power by the highest legitimate political authority for the protection of his own subjects" (p. 78). This authority was essentially reserved as Yahweh's prerogative ; vengeance is not to be taken into private hands. This principle, the reservation of vengeance from the private individual, is a principle of state justice in most if not all state governments today. Mendenhall concludes that "the use and meaning of the verb remained constant from Amarna to King David [fourteenth c. B.C. to tenth c. B.C.] ; the vast difference, consisted in the fact that the king of Egypt as the highest legitimate authority was rejected together with the administrative complex dependent upon him; instead, the God Yahweh now held that executive legitimate power, the actual exercise of which is designated NQM" (p. 78). In biblical thought, Yahweh alone, rather than NE kings and empires, holds the legitimate executive power to execute NAQAM. No private vengeance!

23. Cf. Jonah 4:2.

24. For a biblically oriented, general book against capital punishment, see Gardner C. Hanks, *Against the Death Penalty: Christian and Secular Arguments Against Capital Punishment* (Scottdale, Pa.: Herald Press, 1997); idem, *Capital Punishment and the Bible* (Scottdale, Pa.: Herald Press, 2002).

25. On the *problem* of the "theological center," cf. Elmer A. Martens, *Old Testament Theology* (Grand Rapids: Baker Book House, 1997), 56-66.

26. Cf. Moshe Greenberg, *Ezekiel 1-20, Anchor Bible Dictionary* (New

York: Doubleday & Company, 1983), 18-27.

27. As Thomas L. Thompson writes,

The role of historiography in biblical literature is an issue of wide disagreement among biblical scholars. This debate has taken quite distinct but closely interrelated directions. The definition of historiography has been broadened to include a wider range of narrative prose. Dominant examples of this tendency are both the common perception of biblical narrative as an account of Israel's past, ordered chronologically, and the adoption of J. Huizinga's more theoretical definition of history writing as "the intellectual form in which a civilization renders account to itself of its past". . . : 1) Such broader views of early Israelite historiography allow many modern scholars to understand the documentary sources of the Pentateuch, the final editions of the "Former Prophets," and the compilations of 1-2 Chronicles, Ezra, and Nehemiah as historiographies, and to speak of their authors as historians. In this they define a genre and tradition which stands in direct contrast to the genre and traditions of Mesopotamian, Hittite, and Greek historiography. . . . —*ABD 3*: 207a.

Readers with further interest in this subject should read the rest of Thompson's article and take note of his bibliography.

28. Cf. James E. Brenneman, "Prophets in Conflict: Negotiating Truth in Scripture" in *Peace and Justice shall Embrace:Essays in Honor of Millard Lind*, ed. Ted Grimsrud and Loren L. Johns (Telford, Pa.: Pandora Press U.S.,1999), 49-63.

29. As a boy, I read a children's simplified version of *Pilgrim's Progress* which in my memory still resounds with the contrast of "Sinai's "wind, earthquake, and fire" with the New Testament's "*still small voice.*" While this fearsome view of theophany is certainly true of the Canaanite god Baal, as we shall see from the perspective of the Elijah theophany, it is only vestigially true of Sinai.

30. Cf. James D. G. Dunn, *Jesus, Paul and the Law: Studies in Mark and Galatians* (Louisville: Westminster John Knox Press, 1990).

31. Cf. Eph. 2:8-10.

32. Cf. John Perry, "Not Pledging as Liturgy: Lessons from Karl Barth and American Mennonites on Refusing National Oaths," *The Mennonite Quarterly Review* (Oct. 2002): 431-459.

33. For "the 'Christian Nation' and Other Horrors," see Stephen L. Carter, *The Culture of Disbelief: How American Law and Politics Trivialize Religious Devotion*, (New York: Basic Books, 1993): 83-85.

34. *The Mennonite Encyclopedia*, vol. 3, ed. Harold S. Bender, C. Henry Smith (Scottdale, Pa.: Mennonite Publishing House, et al., 1957), 473b.

35. Menno Simons, *The Complete Writings of Menno Simons, c. 1496-1561*, trans. from the Dutch by Leonard Verduin; John Christian Wenger, ed. (Scottdale, Pa.: Herald Press, 1956), 920-921.

36. For this chapter, I am indebted to the extensive work of James J. Megivern, *The Death Penalty: An Historical and Theological Survey* (New York: Paulist Press, 1997). For the early post-biblical period, see pp. 19-27. Occasionally, after the first sentence of the paragraph crediting him, I may expand on his comment.

Alan Kreider says that to discuss military service in the early church "is to wander into a minefield:" because of difficulties of objectivity of modern writers; some variation of practice in the early church; and the paucity of extant writings on the subject from this period. Kreider examines four early documents of a largely ignored genre which deal with worship, catechesis and pastoral life. His results agree with a "new consensus" about early Christians in the military, though with altered emphases and added nuances. He argues that: "(1) the church orders viewed killing as the big problem for Christians in the legions, not idolatry; (2) the church orders confirm that the pre-Christendom church was divided on Christian participation in the legions; (3) the church orders provide evidence for both discontinuity and continuity on the issue across the centuries, although the deepest continuity, based on John the Baptist's "rule" of Luke 3:14, is between the pre-Constantinian laity and later theologians; (4) the church orders confirm a regional variation in attitude and practice."—Alan Kreider, "Military Service in the Church Orders," *Journal of Religious Ethics* 31.3 (2003) 414-442.1. Arguments in this paper were first presented at Regent's Park College, Oxford, England, May 5, 1999.

37. Megivern, *The Death Penalty*, 51-122.

38. Megivern, *The Death Penalty*, 192-207.

39. Megivern, *The Death Penalty*, 209-228; cf. p. 193.

40. Megivern, *The Death Penalty*, 288-298.

41. The Sinai pericope in the Pentateuch extends from Exod. 19:1–Num. 10:10. Of this, I will deal mainly with the first segment, Exod. 19:1–24:8 (or v. 18). For the importance of the Pentateuch and especially of Sinai/Horeb to the faith community, cf. *ABD 6:* 605, 607.

42. For a history of the study of Near Eastern law, see, Richard Hasse, *Einführung in das Stadium Keilschriftlicher Rechtsquellen* (Wiesbaden: Otto Harrassowitz, 1965) 1-8. The pioneer period of the study of Near Eastern law extended from 1877 A.D. to the end of the century. The second epoch began with the discovery of the Hammurabi stele at Susa (1901/2 A.D.) and extended to the end of World War I. The third epoch began after World War I, stimulated by discoveries from Susa, Mari, Ugarit, Alalakh, and extended to World War II. The fourth epoch began after World War II with the discoveries of the laws of Eshnunna and Lipit-Ishtar. The numerous copies of the Hammurabi code (eighteenth/seventeenth c. B.C.) up to the time of the New Babylonian period (626-539 B.C.), speak for the strong influence of this code throughout the ancient Near East (Hasse, Ibid. pp. 19-20). Driver and Miles say

that there was no comparable comprehensive collection of laws such as that of Hammurabi before the *Digest of Justinian* (see below, *1. Sinai Covenant Code*).

43. Major law collections of the ancient Near East are the Codes of Urnammu (ca. twenty-first century B.C., *ANET*:523-525), Lipit-Ishtar (Sumerian law, nineteenth century B. C., *ANET*:159-161), and Hammurabi (ca. eighteenth century B.C. *ANET*:163-180), the Laws of Eshnunna (ca. nineteenth century A.D., *ANET*:161-163), the Middle Assyrian Laws (twelfth century B.C.?, *ANET*:180-188), the Hittite Laws (fourteenth century B.C.?, *ANET*:188-197), and the Neo-Babylonian Laws (seventh/sixth century B.C., *ANET*:197-198)—cf. *ABD* 4: 242. Old Testament law should be seen as a part of this body of Near Eastern law.

44. Cf. Shalom M. Paul, *Studies in the Book of the Covenant in the Light of Cuneiform and Biblical Law*, (Leiden: E. J. Brill, 1970), 3.

45. For a discussion of the problem of comparing laws between cultures, see Hans Jochen Boecker, *Law and the Administration of Justice in the Old Testament and Ancient East*, trans. Jerry Moiser (Minneapolis: Augsburg Publishing House, l980):15-16. Each collection must be interpreted in terms of the cultures of which it is a part and in terms of its ruling class.

46. The conclusion forms an inclusio with the anticipated covenant (point 1 above), literally placing the entire first segment on law within this covenant envelope. For a more detailed outline, see Brevard S. Childs, *The Book of Exodus,* Old Testament Library (Philadelphia: Westminster Press, 1974), 365. The importance of Child's work is that while he rejects a simple surface (midrashic) approach to the present text for an awareness of a "depth dimension and of the variety of forces which have been at work," he still insists on "interpreting the biblical text before one" (pp. 364-365). I feel, however, that Childs does not emphasize enough the importance of the inclusio in "gaining a perspective of the whole" (p. 365). From the perspective of the final writer-editor(s), this inclusion (the entire segment) means that the Decalogue and Covenant Law Code are to be interpreted in terms of this Covenant Anticipation and Consummation. Cf. Lind, *Ezekiel,* Believers Church Bible Commentary (Scottdale, Pa.: Herald Press, 1996), 381-382. Moses' covenant office, while important, is nevertheless a subsidiary emphasis that should not cloud this main perspective on the relationship of law to covenant.

47. Simplification is always hazardous if one simplifies the research process as well as simplifying communication. On the inaccurate use of the word "code" refer to above, note 16.

48. I have of course made an extensive examination of the other Near Eastern codes and their secondary literature (see above, *Near Eastern Law Codes* and the bibliography). Driver and Miles say, ". . . the conclu-

sion that there was a common customary law throughout the fertile crescent seems irresistible; and this common law was to a considerable extent written law"—G. R. Driver and John C. Miles, *The Babylonian Laws,* vol. 1, Legal Commentary (Oxford: at the Clarendon Press, corrected sheets of 1st ed., 1956, 1960), 9. They also say that there was no equal comprehensiveness of law to that of Hammurabi until the *Digest of Justinian* (sixth c. A.D.; Driver and Miles, 57.)

49. Cf. The Code of Hammurabi, nos. 6, 8; 230; 130; 1, 3; 169—*ANET*:166-282). For its classic position in Near East law, see above, *Near Eastern Law Codes.*

50. For commentaries on the Hammurabi Code, cf. G.R. Driver and John C. Miles, *The Babylonian Laws,* vol. 1, Legal Commentary (Oxford: At the Clarendon Press, corrected sheets of 1st. ed., 1956, 1960) and M.E. J. Richardson, ed., *Hammurabi's Laws* (Sheffield: Sheffield Academic Press, 2000). For the Hammurabi Code as the classic of the ancient Near East, see above.

51. All ancient societies condemned murder; but punishments meted out were different. Biblical law permits kinfolk to take blood revenge "against the slayer or his family members," and is still practiced during the early monarchy (2 Sam. 14:7-11). No money payment may be substituted, for expiation must be made by the life-blood of the murderer (Num. 35:31-34). Two witnesses are required before vengeance could be lawfully made. If holding family members responsible for crimes is an earlier practice, it is later prohibited (2 Kings 14:5-6; Deut. 24:16;). Cities of refuge were established to protect only accidental slayers (Num. 35:9-28; Josh. 20:1-9)—cf. *ABD* 4: 249a. Interpreters who accept biblical authority often regard this demand of death for homicide as evidence of the high value placed on life in the Bible. Others who do not, may regard compensation as practiced by the Hittites as more humane—Ibid. Finally, Ezekiel seems to say that even the shedder of blood who repents will not suffer death (Ezek. 18:10, 21-32)—see chapter p. 108, this volume.

52. See *ANET*: 166. Compensation and blood revenge coexisted "in Assyria in all periods." With the Hittites, however, compensation was the customary penalty. "While there is no case dealing directly with murder in the code of Hammurabi, CH 153 metes out the death penalty to a wife who is an accessory to the murder of her husband. This same offense also led to the death penalty in an earlier Sumerian record of a trial for homicide (*ANET* 542)"—*ABD* 4: 249.

53. Richard Hasse, *Einführung in das Stadium Keilschriftlicher Rechtsquellen* (Wiesbaden: Otto Harrassowitz, 1965). He lists one in the Ur-Nammu and six in the Eshnunna Codes.

54. Hasse, *Einfuhrüng* , 25. He lists nos. 1-3, 6-11, 14-16, 19, 21-22, 26, 33-34, 109, 116, 130, 210, 227, 229-230; cf. *ANET*:166-176. For dragging by oxen, no. 256, *ANET*:177.

55. *ANET*: 172, no. 153. cf. *ABD* 4: 249.

56. *ANET*: 542.

57. *ANET*: 547a.

58. These codes designate money equivalents for loss of body parts instead, Eshnunna # 42-45; Ur-Nammu #15-19, *ANET*: 163a, 524-25. The Hittite penalties for homicide are quite severe, involving the giving of persons in pledge—*ANET iv*: 189. Cf. *ABD* 4: 248.

59. Hasse, *Einführung*, 117. Because of his definitions, this number might be disputed: #116, 196, 197, 200, 210, 229, 230; 25, 153, 192, 193, 194, 195, 218, 226, 253, 282.

60. Richardson, *Hammurabi's Laws* (Sheffield Academic Press, 2000), L 196, 105.

61. Richardson, *Hammurabi's Laws* (L 197), 105.

62. Richardson, *Hammurabi's Laws* (L 200), 105.

63. For a similar case in Hammurabi's Law Code, see L 209, 210, *ANET*: 175.

64. See chapter 1, *Similarities of the Sinai Code to the Hammurabi Code.*

65. *ABD* 4: 321-322.

66. Walter Brueggemann, *Genesis: A Bible Commentary for Teaching and Preaching* (Atlanta: John Knox Press, 1982), 77-88.

67. Claus Westermann, *Genesis 1–11*, trans. John J. Scullion (Minneapolis: Augsburg, 1984), 465.

68. Eugene F. Roup, *Genesis,* Believers Church Bible Commentary (Scottdale, Pa.: Herald Press, 1987), 72.

69. Westermann, *Genesis 1–11*, 467

70. For a critique of biblical and other arguments in support of capital punishment, cf. Christopher D. Marshall, *Beyond Retribution: A New Testament Vision for Justice, Crime and Punishment* (Grand Rapids: Eerdmans, 2001), 214-254.

71. For an extended comparison of ancient Near Eastern with biblical law, refer to *ABD* 4: 242-252.

72. See above, Chapter 1, *Near Eastern Law Codes.*

73. An *inclusio* may be defined as "a literary device in which a section's opening and closing are identical or at least similar. An inclusio by definition ties the end to the beginning; it recapitulates. One might think of an inclusio as a sandwich: material is placed between identical phrases. The effect of such a device is to give unity and emphasis to the passage"—Elmer A. Martens, *Jeremiah.* Believers Church Bible Commentary (Scottdale, Pa.: Herald Press, 1986), 298. For more discussion, see Jack R. Lundbom, *Jeremiah: A Study in Ancient Hebrew Rhetoric,* (Missoula, Mont.: Society of Biblical Literature and Scholars Press, 1975).

74. Cf. Childs, *The Book of Exodus*: 364, for the form-critical comparison of Yahweh's oracle, vs. 3b-6, with many covenant statements in the O.T.

75. For an observation of law within this covenant inclusio, see Dale Patrick. He form-critically identifies the *book of the covenant* mentioned in Exodus 24:7 with the "revelation of covenant law (20:23–23:19)" which "once had a narrative framework consisting of the initial negotiation of the covenant (19:3–8) . . . and the ceremonial ratification of the covenant (24:3-8)"—Patrick, *Old Testament Law* (Atlanta: John Knox Press, 1985), 64. While I welcome this form-critical observation as an important advance in Sinai law studies, I differ from him in that I write from the point of view of a holistic literary method: the final writer-editor(s) places these covenant statements as an inclusio around the entire present pericope, including The Covenant Code and Decalogue. Form criticism makes an important contribution to biblical studies, but because of its hypothetical nature it does not often achieve a consensus; I assume with Brevard S. Childs that "a major purpose of biblical exegesis is the interpretation of the final form of the text. . . ."—Childs, *The Book of Exodus*, 393. For an ancient concept of Moses as prophet see Hosea 12.

76. *Covenant* is the key word in both parts of this inclusio; cf. 24:7-8.

77. For a survey of the traditional literary-critical and tradition-historical approaches to Exod. 19, see Childs, *The Book of Exodus*, 344-350. For a similar survey of 24:1-18, refer to 499-502.

78. There are other types of covenants in the Bible, such as the Noahic, Abrahamic, and Davidic covenants, all of which are similar in that they denote a sworn commitment of God to the relationship; but they lack a comparable human commitment as is found in this Mosaic covenant. Nor do they have the central importance to biblical faith as does this covenant between God and Israel. cf. *ABD* 4: 905-909.

79. In 1954 G. Mendenhall published an article, "Covenant Forms in Israelite Tradition" in *Biblical Archeologist* 17 (1954): 50-76, which sparked a major scholarly debate about the relationship of the Sinai covenant to the ancient Near East international suzerainty treaty forms. While Mendenhall held that the Sinai covenant structure compares with the Hittite suzerainty forms of the twelfth century B.C., today there is growing agreement that the clearest analogy is found in the later book of Deuteronomy to the Assyrian international suzerainty forms (seventh c. B.C.). However, Deuteronomy still exhibits characteristics not found in the Assyrian treaties (Assyrian treaties' lack of appeal to gracious acts of the suzerain, lack of blessings, (*ABD* 1: 1182b;1184b), but which are clearly characteristic of the older Hittite forms. This suggests that while Deuteronomy is strongly influenced by the later Assyrian treaty forms, it still maintains these fundamental differences represented by the older twelfth century Hittite forms. These differences, vital to the concept of biblical faith, thus find their analogies in the twelfth rather than the seventh century B.C. This does not mean that there is necessarily a direct relationship to any of these inter-

national treaties: the fundamental biblical break with all these treaties has to do with the Sinai covenant's rejection of human military power as a basis for covenant in Exod. 19-24. This break speaks so fundamentally to the human condition that for many biblical scholars it is quite intolerable and is denied.

80. For a discussion of the relationship of law and covenant and its significance, see Dale Patrick, *Old Testament Law*, 223-248.

81. While the motive clause, discussed below, is a dependent clause which begins with a relative pronoun, Exod. 19:4 begins as an independent phrase, followed by two conjunctive phrases which further describe what has been seen. In the scholarly guild this is an example of what is called *paranesis* ("preaching"), and is characteristic of Israelite law in contrast to other Near East law. Paranesis was earlier regarded as a relatively late literary phenomenon added to law especially by deuteronomic writers. But Walter Beyerlin has shown that paranesis in this Covenant Code precedes the deuteronomic writing, that it has its origin in an oral rather than literary setting, specifically in the ancient covenant festivals (cf. Exod. 23), and that it likely began in wilderness times: covenant law is law preached (cf. Walter Beyerlin, "Die Paränese in Bundesbuch und ihr Herkunft," ed. Henning Graf Reventlow, *Gottes Wort und Gottes Land* (Göttingen: Vandenhoeck & Ruprecht, 1965), 9-29.

82. I discuss the *motive clause* below. Here Yahweh brings Israel to Sinai rather than his proceeding with Israel from Sinai (cf. Psalms 68:7-10)—Childs, *The Book of Exodus*, 367.

83. Some biblical scholars regard these traditions as arising from the experiences of two separate groups in Israel's history; however, many scholars challenge this separation, holding that the exodus and Sinai are parts "of *one* tradition from the beginning." See *ABD* 4: 906a.

84. In this equivalency, however, the Yahweh covenant qualifies the concept of law. Covenant, unlike contract, does not focus on individual statutes or stipulations, but upon commitment to the well-being of the respective covenant partners to one another, even to the possibility of change of a statute in exceptional situations where it may violate covenant well-being—cf. Elmer A. Martens, *God's Design; a Focus on Old Testament Theology* (Grand Rapids: Baker Book House, 1981), 70.

85. Otto Kaiser sees a unity between Exod. 19:5-6, Gen. 12:2-3 and Isaiah 19:24-25: "I will make of you a great nation, and I will bless you, and make your name great, so that you will be a blessing. I will bless those who bless you, and the one who curses you I will curse, and in you all the families of the earth shall be blessed, Gen.12. // On that day, Israel will be the third with Egypt and Assyria, a blessing in the midst of the earth, whom the Lord of Host has blessed, saying, "Blessed be Egypt my people and Assyria the work of my hands, and Israel my heritage, Isa. 19"—Otto Kaiser, *Der Prophet Isaiah, Kapitel 13-39* (Göttingen: Vandenhoeck & Ruprecht, 1973), 90-99. If Kaiser is correct in this corre-

spondence, then the covenant anticipation of Exodus 19 incorporates within it the concept of the Abrahamic covenant, Israel's vocation to the nations which, to be fulfilled, demands obedience to Mosaic law.

86. For a discussion of the various scholarly viewpoints of "holy war" or "Yahweh war" in the Bible and Israelite history, see Ben C. Ollenburger, "The Theory of Holy War" in Gerhard von Rad, *Holy War in Ancient Israel*, trans. and ed. Marva J. Dawn (Grand Rapids: Eerdmans, 1990), 1-33. For a view of the exodus as the "Paradigm of Holy War in the Old Testament," cf. Millard C. Lind, *Monotheism, Power, Justice: Collected Old Testament Essays* (Elkhart, Ind.: Institute of Mennonite Studies, 1990), 182-196; *idem*, Lind, *Yahweh is a Warrior: The Theology of Warfare in Ancient Israel*, esp. ch. 3; and Waldemar Janzen, *Exodus*. Believers Church Bible Commentary (Scottdale, Pa.: Herald Press, 2000), 463-465. The longer narrative of the exodus sets forth the non-military conflict of this event: faith in the sovereignty of Yahweh over empires, by women who initiate it (Exod. 1:17); the failure of Moses to deliver Israel by violent means (2:11-22); his prophetic commission to deliver Israel from Pharaoh, whom he challenges with only "the staff of God in his hand" (3:1-4:18). Finally, instead of Pharaoh's fear that the Israelite families will "in the event of war, join our enemies and *fight* against us (1:9), the people at the sea are commanded, Yahweh will *fight* for you, and you have only to keep still" (14:14)—cf, Helmut Utzschneider, *Gottes länger Atem: die Exoduserzählung (Ex 1-14) in Ästhetischer und historischer Sicht* (Stuttgart: Verlag Katholisches Bibelwerk, 1996). For an exegesis of the book of Exodus with this perspective, see Waldemar Janzen, *Exodus*.

87. Beginning by quoting John I. Durham, *Exodus* (Waco, Tex.: Word Books, 1987), 263, Waldemar Janzen says of this priestly kingdom: "Durham speaks of 'a kingdom not run by politicians depending upon strength and connivance but by priests depending on Yahweh, a servant nation instead of a ruling nation, . . . a display people, a showcase to the world of how being in covenant with Yahweh changes a people.' Such a role will, of course, make Israel *a holy nation*, a nation set apart in God's service"—Janzen, *Exodus*, 239.

88. Cf. *ABD* 4: 906-907.

89. *ABD* 5: 878-879.

90. For a definition of *inclusio*, see above, *The Radical Revolution of Covenant Law*, footnote 73. This tri-partite division of Prologue, Legal Corpus, and Epilogue is traditional in ancient Mesopotamian law, and is found in fragmented form in the Law Codes of Ur-nammu (2112-2095 B.C.) and Lipit-Ishtar (nineteenth c. B.C.), thus preceding the Hammurabi Code (seventeenth c. B.C.)—*ANET*: 523, 159; 10-12. I follow Shalom M Paul here in comparing this tri-part division with the present form of Exodus 19–24. See his discussion of the problem, *Studies in the Book of the Covenant*, ch. 4, 27-42.

91. Cf. Patrick, *Old Testament Law*, 223, where he calls the covenant Israel's constitution. "Whenever one studies law, sooner or later one encounters constitutional questions, which is to say, questions of authority and sovereignty. Who has authority to make law? How is authority distributed within the legal community? How is the duty to obey justified?"

92. *Anum* is the ancient Mesopotamian sky-god, worshiped especially in the city of Uruk—*ANET*: 164a, note 2.

93. *Enlil* is the ancient Mesopotamian storm-god, executive of the pantheon, worshiped especially in the city of Nippur—*ANET*: 164a, note 4.

94. *Marduk* is the ancient god of the city of Babylon; in Hammurabi's time he mythologically becomes god of the Babylonian empire. Because of the shift in the center of empire to Babylon, Enlil's executive functions are given to him—*ANET*: 164a, note 5.

95. "*ellilut kissat nisi isimusum,* 'they have ordained him to the leadership of the mass of people (Pl)' "—E. J. Richardson, *Hammurabi's Laws* (Sheffield, 2000), 204.

96. The sun-god, *Shamash,* is the ancient god of justice, worshiped especially in the city of Sippar, northern Babylon—*ANET*: 164b, note 11.

97. "*salmat qaqqadim,* 'black on the head,' a figurative expression for mankind"—Richardson, *Hammurabi's Laws,* 277; cf. *ANET*: 164a, note 8.

98. "To light up the land" refers to deeds of justice—cf. above.

99. "The literal translation of the verb phrase is 'to improve the flesh of the people', but it probably has more to do with social reform than medical science"—Richardson, *Hammurabi's Laws,* 31, n. 3.

100. *ANET*: 177b. Richardson translates: "Proper laws established by Hammurabi, the able king, who made the land adopt solid principles and good conduct"—*Hammurabi's Laws,* 119.

101. *ANET*: 178a. Richardson, *Hammurabi's Laws,* 167, 168, *ekutum almattam sutesurim,* "to show justice to the waif and to the widow."

102. *ANET*: 164b.

103. *ANET*:164b.

104. *ANET*:165b. Richardson, *Hammurabi's Laws,* 41, "the king who has made the four parts of the world listen."

105. Hammurabi refers to himself as *king of justice* three times [Richardson, *Hammurabi's Laws,* 120, 121, 124, sar *misarim*]; he refers to justice as *my justice*—*ANET*: 178; to contrast, see Psalms 72:1: "Give the king *your* justice, O God" (emphasis mine).

106. Samuel Greengus, "Law," in *ABD* 4: 245ab.

107. Ibid., *ABD 4*: 244a

108. *ABD 4*: 244b

109. *ABD 4*: 245a

110. *ABD 4*: 245ab

111. For a discussion of this kingship covenant and its tension with

Israelite tradition, cf. Ben Ollenburger, *Zion, City of the Great King: A Theological Symbol of the Jerusalem Cult* (Sheffield: JSOT Press, 1987).

112. See the *Deuteronomistic History* in chapter 3, which deals with the conflict between the kings and the prophetic party.

113. Shalom M. Paul, *Studies*, 33.

114. Cf. *ABD* 6: 383b. Contemporary scholarship does not assign the Decalogue to the time of Moses in its present form, but regards it as a long development, which can no longer be traced. The unity of paranesis (preaching) and law occurred, in my opinion, in the earliest period.

115. *ABD* 6: 384-385.

116. Rabbinic sources give this name to "two black leather boxes containing scriptural passages which are worn by Jews on the forehead and left arm (cf. Matt. 23:5, "Phylacteries" a synonym, *ABD* 5: 368.

117. *ABD* 6: 386.

118. *ABD* 6: 387. For a statement of human rights in the biblical tradition, see Christopher D. Marshall, *Crowned with Glory and Honor; Human Rights in the Biblical Tradition* (Telford, Pa.: Pandora Press U.S., 2001). See also Marshall, *Beyond Retribution*.

119. Cf. Nielsen, *The Ten Commandments in New Perspective: A Traditio-Historical Approach*, trans. D. J. Bourke (Naperville, Ill., 1968). For a critique of such reconstructions, see Patrick, Dale (*Old Testament Law*, Atlanta: John Knox Press, 1985), 39-41.

120. Nielsen, *The Ten Commandments*, 10.

121. See above, *The Radical Revolution of Covenant Law*.

122. Exod. 20:6 is translated variously: cf. RSV, Jerusalem Bible, "but showing steadfast love to thousands"; the NIV, NRSV, *Contemporary English Version* (American Bible Society) follow the lead of the ancient interpretation, Deut. 7:9: "to a thousand generations" (NRSV).

123. *Before Yahweh* is interpreted in many ways by scholars. However that may be, the meaning of this first commandment is clear: Israel is to have no relationship with any divinity other than Yahweh. This exclusivity is "without parallel in the history of religions"—cf. Patrick, *Old Testament Law*, 42; cf. *ABD* 6: 385a.

124. Common throughout the ancient Near East, the idol was the means by which people made contact with the deity. The issue is that Yahweh is not to be manipulated or controlled.

125. Compare this with the U.S. Air Force's "Operation Infinite Justice," a deployment set in motion after the Sept.11 terrorist attacks on the East Coast (*The Goshen News*, Sept. 21, 2001:A-5). Fortunately, this arrogant title was later changed, due not to Christian but to Moslem criticism!

126. Cf. Patrick, *Old Testament Law*: 42. "Although Jewish tradition treats the self-introduction as part of the first commandment, it appears to be an introduction to the entire series of ten. However, it is more closely linked to the first two commandments, since the first per-

son 'Yahweh' is limited to this part of the series. Thus, verses 2-6 constitute a distinct unit of 'I-Thou' address with an introduction (vs. 2) and a conclusion (vs. 5–6). The rest of the Ten Commandments speak of Yahweh in the third person, and this initial unit must bear the weight of establishing the whole as Yahweh's address to his people."

127. See the discussions in *ABD* 6: 385-386; Patrick, *Old Testament Law*, 53-54; Childs, *The Book of Exodus*, 419-421.

128. Cf. *ABD* 6: 386a; Patrick, *Old Testament Law*, 53.

129. Cf. Ollenburger, "Gerhard von Rad's Theory of Holy War," in von Rad, *Holy War*, 1-33.

130. Patrick, *Old Testament Law*, 41.

131. See above, ch. 1, *How the Covenant Inclusio (Exod. 19–24) Contrasts with the Prologue and Epilogue of the Hammurabi Code.*

132. These laws are made up of various types: conditional casuistic case law (*mišpatim*, 21:2-11, etc.); apodictic laws (22:18, 21, 22, 28, etc. [Heb. 17, 20, 21, 27]), participial laws (21:12, 15, 16, 17, etc.), mixed casuistic-apodictic laws (22:25; 26, etc. [Heb. 24, 25], etc.)—cf. Childs, *The Book of Exodus*, 252-254 and *ABD* 4: 252-254.

133. From the form critical point of view, the Covenant Code was originally an independent collection of laws, reflecting the communal life of Israel in its pre-kingship period (cf. Childs, *The Book of Exodus*, 452-453).

134. Cf. Patrick, *Old Testament Law*, 66.

135. For a comparison of biblical with other Near East legal forms, cf. Rifat Sonsino, *Motive Clauses in Hebrew Law, Biblical Forms and Near Eastern Parallels* (Chico: Scholars Press, 1980), 35-39.

136. *Covenant Book*—Exodus 24:7; cf. Childs, *The Book of Exodus*, 451.

137. Cf. Paul, *Studies*, 36.

138. This outline is borrowed from Patrick, *Old Testament Law*, 66-67.

139. Paul, *Studies*, 6-7; this may be compared to the nineteenth century concept of "natural law."

140. *ANET*: 178b.

141. A motive clause may be defined as "a dependant clause or phrase which expresses the motive behind the legal prescription or is an incentive for obeying it"—Sonsino, *Motive Clauses*, 66. I rename this clause the *motive-model clause*, since it is sometimes evident that the clause presents also a model to be followed. Sonsino carefully distinguishes these legal motive clauses from explicative notes and *paranetic statements* (preaching), abundant in Deuteronomy (Sonsion, 68-69). While the motive clause is a dependent clause that is attached "to a legal prescription," *paranesis* ("preaching"), not essentially different in content, is more pervasive (cf. Exod. 20:22b). Along with the motive clause, it is characteristic of Israelite law in contrast to other Near East law. Paranesis was earlier regarded as a relatively late literary phenomenon added to law especially by deuteronomic writers. However, Wal-

ter Beyerlin has shown that paranesis in this Covenant Code precedes the deuteronomic writing, that it has its origin in an oral rather than literary setting, specifically in the ancient covenant festivals (cf. Exod. 23:14-19), and that it likely began in wilderness times: covenant law is law preached (cf. n.81 above).

142. There are a number of other types of motive clauses in the Covenant Code which, though important, may be less pertinent to the death penalty. Sonsino lists the following types of laws with varied motive clauses: Seven cultic-sacral proscriptions of motivated law: against idols (20:22-23); the altar laws (20:25-26), the Sabbatical year (23:10-11a), the Sabbath (23:12); feast of unleavened bread (23:15a); Six proscriptions of humanitarian admonitions and rules of moral conduct: benevolent treatment of stranger, widow and orphan (22:21, 22-24; 29:9); kindness to debtor (22:25-27); four motivated laws of civil legislation, dealing with the rights and obligations of the slave owner (21:8, 21, 26, 27). This makes a total of 17 motivated laws which Sonsino figures as 16% of the laws in the Covenant Code—Sonsino, *Motive Clauses in Hebrew Law,* 87-89.

143. It is thought that in the pre-Israelite period these festivals were separate pastoral and agricultural spring festivals, joined as one festival in Israel. Its celebration of the exodus event is best described in Exod. 12-13.—cf. *ABD* 6: 755-765.

144. Cf. *ABD* 6: 755-765.

145. Uitti (Sonsino, 86) counts four motive clauses as attached to policy law, *The Ten Words* (Exod. 20:2-17): 20:5b-6, 7b, 11, 12b (cf. Eph. 6:2). He does not include Exod. 20:2 because it is an *independent clause* and is thus defined out by its definition according to *form*, though it may have a similar *function*. See above discussion on the Decalogue, vs. 2, 5, 6.

146. Quoted from Lind, *Monotheism,* 66; cf. Sonsino, 86-96.

147. For the concept of rights in the Bible, cf. Christopher D. Marshall, *Crowned with Glory and Honor.* In the Bible, "rights" are grounded theologically, in Yahweh rather than in the state and societal institutions, just as is all covenant law.

148. Linguists tell us that historically, apart from context all so-called "masculine" pronouns are unmarked as to sex, a concept which is true in most (perhaps in all?) languages. In contrast, "feminine" pronouns, even outside of context, are marked as referring to a definite sex. In the English language, the only marked pronoun historically is the third person feminine singular, *she, her,* although in our recent modern period the unmarked pronoun, *he, his, him,* is becoming increasingly marked.

An example of a third person singular unmarked (so-called "masculine") pronoun is, "The *person* who is honest in *his* relationships (historically meaning *his/her*) does not need to fear exposure." The pronoun becomes marked—referring to a male—only in context: "*Jim* who is honest in *his* relationships does not need to fear exposure." The Hebrew pronoun *you* (*'attāh*) is unmarked in Exodus 20:10 and thus refers to either (or both) male and female; if it does not, the mother would be omitted in this passage, which would be inexplicable, since in context *daughter* and *female slave* are included. Since the English *you* is unmarked both sexually and as to number (singular-plural) the NRSV correctly leaves it stand as referring both to father and mother—cf. John Lyons, *Introduction to Theoretical Linguistics* (Cambridge: Cambridge University Press, 1968), 79.

Furthermore, the careful reader will notice that the father/mother, along with son/daughter and male/female slave in this listing are included with *livestock*; this does not mean that ancient Israel did not distinguish between themselves and the animal world (cf. Gen. 1:26; 2:19-20). In my opinion, interpreters who assert otherwise are on questionable ground—cf. Raymond F. Collins in *ABD* 6: 386b. I would concur with Dale Patrick who says that the Sabbath command is addressed to both male and female heads and that "in biblical law a married woman was not considered the property of her husband (Patrick, *Old Testament Law*, 59)." Addressed to the male, the obvious point of the Tenth Commandment is to protect the Hebrew household by curbing the powers of male predators.

149. This early biblical use of the term *Hebrew* is usually regarded as a cognate of the Akkadian term *habiru*, referred to also in Egyptian records of the fifteenth-twelfth centuries B.C., indicating not a nationality but "outsiders of an inferior social position, a class to whom the biblical Hebrew presumably belonged—cf. Millard C. Lind, *Yahweh is a Warrior* (Scottdale, Pa., Herald Press, 1980), 60-61. The Hebrew slave is not like a slave in the modern sense, but more like an indentured servant, that is, one who works out a debt over an extended period of time—cf. Patrick, *Old Testament Law*, 70.

150. Hans Joakim Boecker, 183, emphasis added.

151. For the distinction between Hebrew and foreign slave in ancient Israelite law, cf. Lev. 25:45. But this discrimination against the alien must be weighed with the alien's right to treatment as an Israelite citizen, as indicated in this same Holiness Code (Lev. 19:33:34). Citizenship in the ancient Israel community is determined not by ethnicity, but by religion, and is gained by circumcision (cf. Gen. 17:23). For an article on slavery, see *ABD* 6: 58-65.

152. Cf. Patrick, *Old Testament Law*, 133. He says, "The author desires a slave system so benign that a slave would serve the master of his or her own free will." But this is no mere statement by an "author." It is published covenant law, a proclamation on the authority of the office of Moses (Deut. 5:1; 12:1). It is a directive meant to be obeyed, even if it may be "utopian"—or perhaps better, precisely because it is "utopian."

153. See Patrick *Old Testament Law*, 133 on the "idealistic provisions

of deuteronomic slave provisions" which he feels "would have brought the institution to an end if enforced." Patrick does not reckon with the difficulty of economic life in an ancient society. For many persons a beneficent slave life would be easier (and better) than a life on one's own—cf. Exod. 21:5-6.

154. Eshnunna #14, *ANET*: 524b.

155. Hammurabi #15, *ANET*: 166-167

156. In the legal portion of the Hammurabi Code, interhuman laws pertaining to the ruling classes—which *have to do with the structure of the justice system*—logically come first (*awelum, ANET*: 166a; cf. note 39). In the Covenant Code, on the other hand, divine-human laws logically come first; for *in this code such laws have to do with the structure of human justice* (Exod. 20:22-26). In this way, covenant law, administered from the viewpoint of the tabernacle, attempts to guard against the vested interests of the ruling classes (cf. Ps. 72:1). While one might say that in Israel the Levites and priests, in charge of worship, also tend to be "ruling class," yet the Levites and priests have no tribal territory, but are limited to towns with their pasture lands, towns which are distributed among the various tribal territories. Yahweh is their portion (cf. Josh. 13:8–22:9, esp. chap. 21. They are divested of capital property. For a visionary reform of this assignment, cf. Ezek. 45:1-5).

157. Paul Hanson, "The Theological Significance of Contradiction within the Book of the Covenant," in *Canon and Authority: Essays In Old Testament Religion And Theology*, ed. George W. Coats and Burke O. Long; with contributions by Peter R. Ackroyd et al. Festschrift für Zimmerli (Philadelphia: Fortress Press, 1977): 114.

158. For a discussion of the Cain-Abel narrative, see above, ch. 1, *Similarities of the Sinai Code to the Hammurabi Code,* and ch. 4, *Fifth Antithesis: The Law of Retaliation.*

159. For how covenant law permeates and is often the hidden subject of a narrative, cf. David Daube, *Studies in Biblical Law* (Cambridge: Cambridge University Press, 1947), 1-61.

160. Hosea 1-3. This is discussed at some length in chapter 3, below.

161. See discussion below on Hosea 1–3; 11; Ezekiel 18, etc.

162. *ANET*: 178a.

163. Cf. *ANET*: 163-180; esp. 177-180.

164. "Mari (Texts)," *ABD* 4: 529-538.

165. Cf. Jorg Jeremias, *Hosea und Amos, Studien zu den Anfängen den Dodekapropheton,* (Tübingen: J .C. B. Mohr Paul Siebeck, 1996), 22-27; 104-107.

166. This begins with Moses, is recognized as a movement especially in the time of Samuel, and continues into the exile period and after.

167. A still widely influential hypothesis on the date of their writing, though presently under assault, was proposed by Martin Noth in his *Überlieferungsgeschichtliche Studien,* 1943 (Eng. trans., The Deuterono-

mistic History, *Journal for the Study of the Old Testament* Sup. 15 (Sheffield: JSOT Press, 1967).On the basis of similar language and theology of history used throughout, he concluded that essentially the present five books, Deuteronomy, Joshua, Judges, Samuel and Kings form one unity.

According to Noth, most of the material of the last four books, written after the final episode, 2 Kings 25:27-29—Nebuchadnezzar's release from prison and elevation of King Jehoiachin, 563 B.C.—was appended to the original core of Deuteronomy. This deuteronomic core provided the historian with his theology of history for the entire work: blessing for obedience to the law and curse for disobedience. European scholars still favor this exilic date, while American scholars favor a pre-exilic date toward the end of King Josiah's reign (640-609 B.C.), a date suggested by Frank Moore Cross, *Canaanite Myth and Hebrew Epic* (Cambridge, Mass.: Harvard University Press, 1973), 274-89. (This assumes that the materials after that date were added, sometime after Jehoiachin's release from prison (2 Kings 25:27-29).

For this book, I provisionally accept the date suggested by Frank Cross with the hypothesis that the deuteronomic historian may have had at hand various earlier editions of Israel's history, or portions thereof, which he or later editors incorporated into the final work. I assume that the work was finally completed in the exilic period. The division of the *Former Prophets* into the six present books may be due to the optimal length of the ancient scroll. My interpretive method is a holistic literary one, relating the parts to the Deuteronomistic History in its final canonical form: Joshua–2 Kings (minus Ruth), with Deuteronomy, the final book of the Pentateuch, as its ruling social-theology of history (cf. David Noel Freedman, "Pentateuch," in *The Interpreters Dictionary of the Bible*, vol. 3, ed. George Arthur Buttrick (Nashville: Abingdon Press, 1962), 716ff.

168. This chart is my work, taken from *Ezekiel*, 382.

169. The Elijah-Elisha materials extend from 1 Kings 17 to 2 Kings 13:21. Critics are far from a consensus on the growth of the Elijah-Elisha tradition, as well as its insertion into its larger context, the Deuteronomistic History (see above). Susanne Otto, tracing the complicated and contradictory results of this scholarly criticism, says that G. H. Steck is essentially in agreement with George Fohrer, though more complex: the process began in the life-time of Elijah by the formation of individual narratives and was largely finished by the end of the ninth century B.C. The sociological setting of this early literary activity was the prophetic schools of Elisha, found at Jericho, Gilgal, and Bethel (cf. 2 Kings 2:15-25; 4:38-44). Skeptics of this early dating find the monotheistic confession (1 Kings 18:39) and the polemic against idols (1 Kings 18:27) as hardly thinkable in pre-exilic times, at least not before Hosea—cf. Susanne Otto, *Jehu, Elia and Elisa,, Die Erzählung von der*

Jehu-Revolution und die Komposition der Elia-Elisa-Erzählungen (Stuttgart: Kohlhammer, 2002), 14-25. But those critics who tend to date Israel's literary activity more or less entirely in the exilic period and later, may need to revise their ideas somewhat in light of the literary achievements in Israel's earliest Near East environment as well as in light of Israel's early poetry: Gen. 49; Exod. 15:1-18; Num. 23-24; Deut. 33; Judg. 5; Deut. 32, etc. For a discussion, see David Noel Freedman, "Prolegomena" in George Buchanan Gray, *The Forms of Hebrew Poetry* (New York: KTAV Publishing House, 1972), vii-xlvi.

170. Cf. Elijah's experience with Moses in Exod. 20:18; cf. 20:22.

171. Jeremias states that Hosia, eighth century B.C., begins the prophetic practice of using the *Baal* divinity as a cipher for all non-Israelite gods and Israel's failed relationship to Yahweh and divine worship. cf. Jorg Jeremias, 86-96.

172. Stephen W. Holloway, "Kings, Books of," in *ABD* 4: 76.

173. Cf. Otto, 256, my translation.

174. By regarding the Elijah of the drought legend as the only reliable historical core of the Elijah narratives, Marsha White challenges the biblical tradition that there was a mid-ninth century populist uprising against the Omride dynasty. Instead, she evaluates Jehu's act not as a broad based populist uprising but a narrow based military *coup d' etat*—Marsha C. White, *The Elijah Legends and Jehu's Coup* (Atlanta: Scholars Press, 1997). This revisionist view raises again the question of the biblical view of the prophets' place in Israel's history. For a more positive view, besides the references referred to above, see Walter Dietrich, *David, Saul, und die Propheten: das Verhältnis von Religion und Politik nach des prophetischen Überlieferungen vom frühesten köningtum in Israel* (Stuttgart: W. Kohlhammer, 1987); Antony F. Campbell, *Of Prophets and Kings, a Late Ninth-Century Document (1 Samuel 1-2 Kings 10),* (Washington, D.C.: The Catholic Biblical Association of America, 1986).

175. Like Omri, Jehu is a military officer who assassinates his king and establishes his own dynasty (cf. *ABD* 3: 670-673).

176. On Carmel and Elijah's contest with the Baal prophets, see *ABD* 1: 874-875.

177. Susanne Otto sees the origin of the narrative, "Elijah on Mount Horeb" (1 Kings 19) and its present placement in the Book of Kings as happening in the fifth century B.C. , though she accepts the origin of many other narratives of this prophet as nearly contemporary with his ninth century ministry. She traces this development as follows:

(1) Around 560 B.C. the Deuteronomistic editors established the basic text of their Deuteronomistic History (DH). For this climactic epoch of their work, from Ahab to Jehu (1 Kings 16:29–2 Kings 10:36), the intention of these editors was to witness to the power of the word of Yahweh, spoken by the prophet Elijah, to determine history. At the same time, they anchored the topic, "The Cultic Disruption of the Baal

Cult and the Subsequent Cultic Reform" in the history of the Northern Kingdom [before its demise in 722 B.C.]

(2) In Otto's view, not long afterward the previously edited "Collection of the Prophetic War Narratives" (1 Kings 20:1-34; 2 Kings 6:24-30, 32a, 33abb; 7:1, 3-16) was inserted by these DH editors into their basic text. This collection was quite sympathetic with the DH text: the death of kings according to prophetic judgments were decisive historical moments.

(3) The two following layers of tradition, the First and Second Post-Deuteronomistic Editions in the Sector of the Elijah Narratives, Otto also ascribes to prophetic circles; however, in their intention, they are very distant from the DH writers. Otto holds that with the insertion of the First Edition of the Elijah Collection into the DH at the new beginning after the exile, the concept of the DH of the depravity of the Omrides was destroyed, in favor of an optimistic conception of the effectiveness of a "didactic" prophecy, one of judgment leading to repentance, by a combination of judgment as purification and a demonstration of Yahweh's unique divinity, and by the notorious sinner Ahab's basic adaptability.

(4) Finally, Otto's hypothesis holds that only in the fifth century was the Elijah composition supplemented by the narrative , "Elijah on Mount Horeb;" simultaneously, the "Elisha Biography" and the Narrative of Hasael's Usurpation of the Throne was inserted into the enlarged DH. Otto's thesis is that by tracing back the political interference of disaster prophecy to Elijah's commission which issued from the theophany (1 Kings 19:11-16) and by the demonstration of the many life affirming works of Elisha, the prophecy of the Elijah-Elisha Cycle was given a secure basis in the history of Israel, a prophecy which justified the violence of Jehu's revolution—Otto, *op. cit.*: 248.

For a more positive historical view of 1 Kings 19 and its meaning in the early Elijah Cycle, cf. John Gray, *I and II Kings; A Commentary* (Philadelphia: Westminster Press, 1975), 373-374, 405-414.

178. Cf. Alan J. Hauser and Russell Gregory, *From Carmel to Horeb* (Sheffield: The Almond Press, 1990), 61.

179. Few of the many historical-critical works which I have examined recognizes this common rhetorical device of both Old and New Testaments. See, Jack R. Lundbom, *A Study in Ancient Hebrew Rhetoric; Martens, Jeremiah,* 298. An example of historical-critical resistance to rhetorical criticism is Ernst Würthwein's complaint in "Elijah at Horeb: 'Reflections on 1 Kings 19:9-18'" in *Studium zur Deuteronomistischen Geschichtswerk* (Berlin: Walter de Gruyter, 1994), 141, "It is clear, at the first glance, that the text can scarcely be said to be in order." What he means to say is that the text is not in *linear* order! In his view, J. Wellhausen "restores" the original text by omitting vv. 9b-11a; George Fohrer regards vv. 9b-11aa as a dogmatic gloss, meant "to reduce the

significance of, or even to replace, the description of the theophany"— Quoted by Würthwein, 141. John Gray is more literary in his approach by observing that "such repetition is well known in the saga convention and may be deliberate . . . "—John Gray, 405.

180. The meaning of Elijah's theophany is disputed. See below, *Theophany at Horeb, Three Negatives and a Whisper*. In my opinion, its meaning for the biblical editor-writer(s) can be determined only by taking seriously the literary structure of 1 Kings 19:9b-14 and by relating it to its immediate context, 1 Kings 17-19, and to its larger context, the Deuteronomistic History. From a literary point of view, "it is safe to say that the various stories and traditions in 1 Kings 17-19, whatever their origin, have not been loosely assembled and simply placed together in a roughly chronological order, but rather have been carefully and artfully woven into a narrative tapestry of considerable power"—Hauser and Gregory, 82. For a discussion of the relationship between historical-critical research and literary criticism, see Ibid.: 149-150.

181. The issue underlying the narrative of Naboth's vineyard is, who is the owner of land in Israel and who may dispose of it. In Israel, land is owned by Yahweh, and according to Joshua 13–19, was distributed for use to the families of the various tribes by Joshua and the priesthood soon after the occupation. In contrast, Canaanite kingship, as witnessed by the Ras Shamra texts, made grants of land to certain classes and persons, who thus became royal dependants—cf. John Gray, 439; Würthwein, 155-177; *ABD 3*: 148b.

182. Quote from David Rhoads, "Zealots" in *ABD 6*: 1044a.

183. *ABD 3*: 306, reported by C. L. Seow, "Hosts, Lord of" in *ABD 3*: 305a.

184. Hauser and Gregory, 67; emphasis added.

185. Partly because historical-critical scholars often do not acknowledge this literary structure of 1 Kings 19:9b-14, they have been largely unsuccessful in interpreting the meaning of the theophany in vv.11-13a. Ernst Würthwein writes, "Thus it is impossible to consider as successful either the older or the more recent attempts to interpret the theophany theologically and to relate it to its context. The fact that these attempts fail repeatedly seems to me to show that we are dealing here with a profound disturbance of the narrative and that we must use more radical means to recover the original course of the story"— Würthwein, 147. Since in his opinion "the commentators have succeeded only in making a link between the theophany and its context by means of interpretations more or less forced" (Hauser and Gregory, 147), and since the repetition of Elijah's lament, vv. 13b-14, is a "stylistic device" which *ends an interpolation* "with a statement which often corresponds word for word with that which occurs at the point where the original text is interrupted" (Ibid.,149, quoting favorably E. Hirsch), Würthwein concludes: "We are therefore justified in holding vv. 11-14

to be alien to the original story." He then shows how "The text of the scene at Horeb [vv. 9-18] then reads in its original form" (Ibid.,149-150), omitting vv. 11-14, and altering some of the others. It is interesting that Würthwein, quoting Hirsch, here recognizes the stylistic device of literary criticism, the inclusion, whose center may highlight its literary context, but regards it as indicating a later interpolation.

186. See Theodore Hiebert, "Theophany in the Old Testament," in *ABD* 6: 505-511 and Leah Bonner, *The Stories of Elijah and Elisha as Polemics Against Baal Worship* (Leiden: E. J. Brill, 1968).

187. C. L. Seow, 305*a*; cf. *ANET* 1969:130*b*-131*a*.

188. In Job 4:12-16, Eliphaz describes the human experience of divine communication. The description ends with *demama weqol 'esma'*: "silence, and a voice I heard," my verbatim translation. If I understand him correctly, O. H. Steck agrees with this interpretation, though with qualifications. Steck writes, "Yahweh is set against the deities of the world around and against the ways in which they manifest themselves—Yahweh, who manifests himself in his word to the prophets, and who works through them (vv. 15-18)," *Überlieferung und Zeitgeschichte in den Elia-Erzählungen*, (Neukirchen-Vluyn: Verlag des Erziehungsvereins, 1968), 118—quoted from Würthwein, 118. The prophetic function of Moses as lawgiver is recognized in Exodus 18:16, 23 in the greater matters of *the statutes and instructions of God;* minor case laws, however, are the decisions of the judges themselves (Exod. 18:22). Law and prophecy are closely joined.

189. Georg Fohrer, *Elia, AThANT* (Zurich: Zwingli Verlag, 1957), 89, quoted from Würthwein, *op. cit.*:142, n. 7. While this statement is insightful, it would be strengthened by recognizing the Elijah theophany as a revaluation of Sinai. Citing Jorg Jeremias, *Theophanie. Die Geschichte einer alttestamentlichen Gattung,* (Neukirchen-Vluyn: Verlag des Erziehungsvereins, 1965), 113f., Würthwein says that "three kinds of answers have been given to this question . . .: (1) a natural or aesthetic interpretation which sees the theophany purely in sensuous and pictorial terms (Wellhausen) or sees it as expressing the divine majesty of God, released from all natural phenomena (Gressmann); (2) a moralizing explanation, according to which Elijah is told to fight with inner weapons (Volz); (3) a far-reaching spiritualizing interpretation which finds, among other things various indications in the theophany of Yahweh's true spiritual nature." Würthwein is probably correct in rejecting all of these—Würthwein, 142.

190. Cf. Ben Ollenburger, "Gerhard von Rad's Theory of Holy War" in Gerhard von Rad, *Holy War in Ancient Israel*, 1-33.

191. For a more general survey of Israel's clash with these cultures, cf. Leah Bonner.

192. Jeremias, *Theophanie*, 115, quoted by Würthwein, *Studien*, 143. Würthwein quotes Jeremias to argue against his view. He not only

elides the theophany as secondary, but says, "That 'Yahweh was not in the storm, the fire, the earthquake' should really be understood in the sense: 'he was not (yet) in them'" (Jeremias, n. 12). But O. H. Steck writes correctly, Yahweh is set against the deities of the world around and against the ways in which they manifest themselves—Yahweh, who manifests himself in his word to the prophets, and who works through them (vv. 15-18 in *Überlieferung*, 118—quoted by Würthwein, *Studien*, 141).

193. Martin Noth, *The History of Israel*, (New York: Harper and Brothers, 1958), 2-3.

194. This includes both Sinai covenant law (Exod. 19:3–20:24:8) and its discussion in 1 Kings 19:9-14.

195. Deuteronomic law. cf. Moshe Weinfeld, "Deuteronomy," in *ABD 2*: 169-170.

196. This title was first used by Augustine (A.D. 354-430) in his commentary on the Sermon—*ABD 5*: 1106.

197. There are in the Bible a few isolated laws decreed by kings (1 Sam. 30:24-25), and exhortations to obey the teachings and laws of parents (Prov. 1:8; 6:20; Jer. 32:11, etc.); cf. Greengus, "Law," *ABD 4*, 244b. Likely it was understood that all such laws are to be brought "before God" (Exod. 18:19-20). The problem of law is not essentially different from that of genuine and false prophecy (cf. 1 Kings 22). See Jeremiah's complaint about "the false pen of the scribes" (Jer. 8:8-9).

198. Cf. Gerhard von Rad, *The Message of the Prophets* (New York: Harper & Row, 1967), 227-228.

199. Gray, *I and II Kings*, 410. But such an important commentator as Georg Fohrer is not to be dismissed quickly (see Fohrer quote and note 189 above).

200. See below.

201. Though the Masoretic text indicates a break between 1 Kings 19:14 and 15, suggesting perhaps that the ancients did not relate vv. 15ff. immediately to the theophany, I ignore this break, as do most modern translations.

202. Hazael's revolution follows Jehu's rather than precedes it—Gray, *I and II Kings*, 412.

203. On the basis of an inscription newly found at Tel Dan, Suzanne Otto suggests that Jehu's revolution was undergirded by the Aramaic king, Hazael—Otto, *op. cit.*, 101. Was Elisha therefore guilty of treason by this prophetic anointing? Cf. Amos 7:10-17. From the prophetic viewpoint the king is guilty of treason against Israel's Ruler, Yahweh.

204. Cogan and Tadmor, *II Kings* (Garden City, N.J.: Doubleday & Company, Inc., 1988), 117-122.

205. See above, Theophany at Horeb.

206. Würthwein, *Studium*, 150-151.

207. Susanne Otto differs with Würthwein, holding that the theo-

phany was a part of the original text of the chapter but comes to much the same conclusion as to what is pivotal in the Deuteronomistic History as presented by the present text. Following E. Blum, she states that "the weight of the text does not lie on the theophany—the theophany in itself does not deal with the crises of prophecy in Israel, *for the lament of Elijah remains the same (v. 14; cf. v. 10)*—but on the new [i.e. vv. 15-18], since the task for Elijah issued from the theophany"—Otto, *Elia und Elisa*, 185, my translation, emphasis added. Thus, like many historical-critical scholars, Otto fails to recognize the *inclusion*, a devise which, among other things, emphasizes the climactic character of what lies at the center, and is commonly recognized by literary scholars—cf. above, "Theophany at Horeb."

208. Stamm, *op. cit.*, 334, quoted from Würthwein, *Studium.*, 144, emphasis added. While Würthwein welcomes "Stamm's endeavor to bring out again the inner connection between the description of the theophany and the statements connected with it in vv. 15f." (Ibid.), he criticizes Stamm's concept that the seven thousand are "the real object of Yahweh's activity, the sphere where he is present," and, "by contrast, Elijah's spectacular tasks represent only transitional stages, acts of judgment which forward this aim." Würthwein questions

> whether it is in keeping with the faith of the Old Testament to find these distinctions in history, as though Yahweh were not present in judgment as truly as in salvation. If I am right, then vv. 15-17 answer the doubts and questionings about what Israel experienced at the hands of Hazael, Jehu and Elisha. The answer is that what takes place occurs not just by permission of Yahweh, but is in fact set in motion by Yahweh. He is therefore wholly and intrinsically involved in it, just as clearly as he is in the salvation of the seven thousand. The sentence, 'Yahweh is also the originator of these (i.e. the acts of judgment) but they are not the sphere of his actual presence,' does not seem to me to take this into account; it is challenged by the whole Old Testament view of history. (145)

My question is this: Though the Old Testament takes judgment seriously as Yahweh's action, does it represent that judgment is on the same level as salvation? Even Israel's ancient poetry sees judgment against Israel as disciplinary, and that beyond judgment Yahweh *will vindicate his people, have compassion on his servants* (Deut. 32, esp. vv. 26ff., emphasis added). And I would claim this: Elijah's experience of theophany speaks not in general about God, judgment and salvation, but specifically about how the theophanic experience of Moses and the people at *Mount Sinai* is to be interpreted. See above, "Theophany at Horeb: Three Negatives and a Whisper."

209. Cf. Lind, "Recognition Formula" in *Ezekiel*, 380-381.

210. Hauser and Gregory, *From Carmel to Horeb*, 138.

211. Exod. 33:12-23, Moses at Sinai; cf. Jer. 7:16; 11:14; Ezek. 11:13.

212. Otto, *Jehu, Elia und Elisa*, 185, note 161.

213. Martin Noth held that the intention of the DH is to announce to the exiles their final end and judgment, leaving them no hope, a concept which today is considered inadequate. Gerhard von Rad found an intent of hope in the Messianic promise, while Hans Walter Wolff convincingly argues that the main intention of DH is to bring the exiles to repentance—H. W. Wolff, "The Kerygma of the Deuteronomic Historical Work," in *The Vitality of Old Testament Traditions*, eds. Walter Brueggemann and Hans Walter Wolff (Atlanta: John Knox Press, 1976), 83-100).

214. Gerhard von Rad, *Studies in Deuteronomy*, trans. David Stalker (Chicago: Henry Regnery Company, 1953), 91: "Refusal to enter into the great problems of internal politics is not to be explained simply as incapacity on the part of the Deuteronomist. What the Deuteronomist presents is really a history of the creative word of Jahweh. What fascinated him was, we might say, the functioning of the divine word in history. And so, in reality, there lies in this limitation a tremendous claim. The decisive factor for Israel does not lie in the things which ordinarily cause a stir in history, nor in the vast problems inherent in history, but it lies in applying a few very simple theological and prophetic fundamental axioms about the nature of the divine word.

And so it is only this word of Yahweh that gives continuity and aspiration to the phenomenon of history, which unites the varied and individual phenomena to form a whole in the sight of God. Thus the Deuteronomist shows with exemplary validity what saving history is in the Old Testament: that is, a process of history which is formed by the word of Yahweh continually intervening in judgment and salvation and directed towards a fulfillment." This relation of word to history is analogous in nature not essentially to the storm, but to the seed which, dropped into the ground, brings forth fruit (Isa. 28:23-27; 55:11-12), as 1 Kings 19:11-12 intimates.

215. For the concept of miracle as a sign or wonder which points up the future way that the community of faith will take, see Yair Zakovitch, "Miracle" (OT) in *ABD 4*: 845.

216. Cf. Jesus and the fig tree, Mark 11:12-14.

217. For this translation, see Cogan and Tadmor, *II Kings*, 54.

218. For a discussion of Solomon's fiscal system and districts, and their oppressive consequences, see Gray, *II Kings*, 134-135.

219. Cf. above, *Elisha, Shepherd to the "seven thousand."*

220. Hardin Craig, *Shakespeare* (Chicago, et. al.: Scott, Foresman and Company, 1931) , 932.

221. On the Arameans, see A. Kirk Grayson, *ABD 4*: 740-741.

222. In 853 and 735 B.C. Israel and Damascus are involved in western military alliances against Assyria—Winfried Thiel, "Ahab," *ABD 1*: 101a; *ABD 5*: 215a .

223. This vocabulary is designed not only to claim that the fourth element of the theophany is upon a quite different plane from the first three, but that this asymmetry is first reflected in the statement of covenant law at Sinai, in the tension between motive-model clause of Yahweh's deliverance from Egypt and the death penalty still attached to much of Israel's technique law.

224. Cf. Matt. 26:52.

225. Otto, *Jehu, Elia und Elisa,* 101, my translation. cf. notes 420-429.

226. H. Winkler, 170-175. Winkler touched off a discussion by German Old Testament scholars on the prophets' political message which stretched across much of the twentieth century, all of whom rejected Winkler's view. For a survey of this discussion, see Hans-Joachim Kraus, *Prophetie und Politik* in *Theologische Existenz Heute* series (München: Chr. Kaiser Verlag, 1952).

227. See Kraus *Prophetie und Politik.* He cites Paul de Lagarde, *Deutsche Schriften,* 4 auf.: 224, as having the opposite understanding of the political position of the Hebrew prophet as does Winkler (cf. above, note 227). de Lagarde holds that for the first time in history there burned in these prophets the purest flame of love for the fatherland; they were passionately patriotic.

228. Cogan and Tadmor, *II Kings,* 117-118.

229. Cogan and Tadmor, *II Kings,* 118.

230. Cf. Jeremiah 35.

231. 2 Kings 9-10; cf. Cogan and Tadmor, *II Kings,* 120.

232. For a statement on the DH and its relation to the Elijah-Elisha material, see above, notes on *The Law and the Prophets* and *The Baal Apostasy of the Omride Dynasty.*

233. See above, Chapter 1, *The Decalogue, Exodus 20:2-17* for a discussion of the relationship between the first and second commandments and the structure for justice in Israel. We have just discussed the emphasis on social justice in the Elisha stories.

234. It is interesting that we seem to have little problem understanding the Baalistic economic system, but need to have the Israelite system explained. May this be because our economic system is Baalistic?

235. Cf. John Gray, *I and II Kings,* 435: "We should retain the passage as a prophetic version of a significant tradition of Elijah and Ahab, which retains, though not literally in every detail, a true reflection of the consequences of the policy of the house of Omri to effect a synthesis of Israelite and Canaanite tradition, of which the marriage of Ahab and Jezebel was symptomatic."

236. John Gray, *I and II Kings,* 439.

237. Cf. Lind, *Monotheism,* 215-226.

238. For modern day traditions where power is voluntarily given up, witness the surrender of an incumbent of a democratic state who loses an election.

239. See Terrence Pendergast, "The Trial of Jesus," *ABD 6*, 660-663. For a comparison of the trials of Jesus and Jeremiah, see Elmer A. Martens, *Jeremiah*. Believers Church Bible Commentary (Scottdale, Pa.: Herald Press, 1986), 170.

240. The death sentence is a functioning reality in Israel's ancient courts—and these legal assemblies can be manipulated. In Jeremiah's case, "the officials and all the people" declared, "This man does not deserve the sentence of death . . ." (Jer. 26:16). Jeremiah's like-minded prophet Uriah, however, did not fare so well. Extradited from Egypt where he had fled from the king's wrath because "he had prophesied against this city and against this land in words exactly like those of Jeremiah," he was struck down with the sword by King Jehoiachin who threw his dead body into the burial place of the common people (Jer. 26:20-23).

241. For the authority of the prophet as bearer of God's word on the course of history in the thought of the DH, cf. Gerhard von Rad, *Deuteronomium-Studien*, 2 Auflage, 1948, trans. David Stalker (Chicago: Henry Regnery Company, 1953). Von Rad's widely accepted thesis is that the Old Testament is a historical book, which presents a history effected by God's word. The first way in which history is effected, according to this analysis of the DH, is by obedience to God's word of law, especially as presented in the book of Deuteronomy. This is evident in the narrative of Naboth's Vineyard where Ahab is confronted by the prophet Elijah with the violation of Yahweh's law (cf. also Nathan to David, 2 Sam. 12:9). A second way in which history is effected in the DH according to von Rad is by prophetic promise and fulfillment (2 Sam. 7:13; 1 Kings 8:20; cf. von Rad, 78). Although Ernst Würthwein challenges von Rad's second way in which history is effected, I think not successfully ("Prophetisches Wort und Geschichte in den Königsbuchern, Zu einer Gerhard von Rads," in *Studien zum Deutonomistischen* , 80-92). For example, Jehoiachin's release from prison is best explained as included in the DH because of that prophetic promise (2 Kings 25:27-29).

242. See above note.

243. See above, *Naboth's Vineyard, a Flashback, 1 Kings 21.*

244. See above, *Jehu's Blood Bath at Jezreel, 2 Kings 9:1–10:31.*

245. Cf. 2 Kings 10:32-36.

246. Cogan and Tadmor, *II Kings*, 122.

247. See Francis I. Andersen and David Noel Freedman, *Hosea*, Anchor Bible (Garden City, N.J.: Doubleday & Company, Inc., 1980), 176-182.

248. For limited blessing and its possible relation to limited retribution, see Cogan and Tadmor, *II Kings*, 116, comment on 2 Kings 10:30.

249. Cf. Isa. 45:4-5.

250. Cf. James E. Brenneman, "Prophets in Conflict: Negotiating

Truth in Scripture" in *Peace and Justice Shall Embrace, Power and Theopolitics in the Bible*, editors, Ted Grimsrud and Loren L. Johns, (Telford, Pa.: Pandora Press U.S.,1999), 49-63.

251. Cf. Cogan and Tadmor, *II Kings*, 3.

252. *ABD 3*: 292b.

253. Cf. Andersen and Freedman, *Hosea*, 220.

254. Cf. Andersen and Freedman, *Hosea,*: 231.

255. Hans Walter Wolff, *Hosea*, trans. Gary Stransell (Philadelphia: Fortress Press), 61.

256. For a discussion on the dates of Amos's visionary experiences, see Francis I. Andersen and David Noel Freedman, *Amos*. Anchor Bible (New York: Doubleday, 1989), 183. Though Amos speaks first of all *concerning Israel*, Freedman suggests that the oracles may have been delivered to the various nations by the prophet himself—cf Andersen and Freedman, *Amos*, 232. If he speaks to Israel only, then it may be to remind Israelites of their covenant responsibility to the nations, , including perhaps that they deliver the message to them.

257. Most modern critical scholars have doubted the originality of one or more of the oracles against the nations around Israel; Andersen and Freedman, however, considers all eight oracles as original—Andersen and Freedman, *Amos*, 206-211. For Carmel as a symbol of the entire region, see Ibid., 228.

258. For *fire* as a mythic term and directly sent by God, cf. Andersen and Freedman, *Amos*, 239.

259. For a discussion of the following atrocities, see Andersen and Freedman, *Amos*: of *Damascus*: 239; *Gaza*: 258-259; *Tyre*: 261; *Edom*: 264-265; *Ammonites*: 281; *Moab*: 287-288. For a comprehensive statement, see p. 277.

260. Andersen and Freedman, *Amos*, 288, on Moab.

261. Andersen and Freedman, *Amos*, 231

262. Andersen and Freedman, *Amos*, 232-233; 916-917.

263. Robert G. Boling regards Joshua 24:1-28 as stemming "ultimately from a great revolutionary gathering at Shechem . . . ." He says that in it "we see a clear and somewhat different image of the hero of the conquest come into focus. Yahweh won far more towns with Joshua in the role of ambassador than with Joshua as field commander of the militia." He dates the first edition of the book of Joshua to Josiah's reign (dtr 1) and the final edition after the collapse of the state: "The Josianic attempt to use the power of the throne in reactivating the authority of Moses collapsed with the death of the king himself. As the reality of exile became inevitable, it was time for persons to do once again what the founding fathers did at Shechem: Choose!"—Robert G. Boling, *Joshua*. Anchor Bible (Garden City, N.J.: Doubleday & Company, Inc., 1982), 543-544.

264. See discussion of Ollenburger's work above, Preface and Chap-

ter 1, *How Covenant Inclusio (Exod. 19–24) Contrast with Prologue and Epilogue of the Hammurabi Code.*

265. Cf. Lind, "Recognition Formula," in *Ezekiel*, 380-381.

266. Cf. Andersen and Freedman, *Amos*, 231-232 where they question that these " 'acts of rebellion' were just offenses against conscience in days long before any declarations of human rights as such . . . ." To this I agree. But may the specific violations of the nations be against Yahweh's covenant with Israel whose behavior the nations were then to emulate (compare Amos 3:9 and Isaiah 2:2-5) rather than against a commercial treaty such as Israel may have made with Tyre (1 Kings 9:10-14)? This may have been qualified by Yahweh's covenant-law type of treaty, but under Solomon it was more likely based on a power treaty *like the nations.* However that may be, the radical prophet Amos more probably reaches back to a pre-kingship memory of a Yahweh-Israelite model—how can one say, except that his critique seems to mesh adequately with Israel's vocational covenant oracle of Exod. 19:3-6. See Ezekiel's critique against treaties with foreign nations, against power-oriented treaties that are incompatible with Yahweh's covenant with Israel. (Ezek. 23; cf. Lind, "No Military Alliances" and "The New Order," in *Ezekiel,* 198-203). Compare Ezekiel's critique with the Maccabean treaty with Rome (*1 Maccabees* 8; cf. Thomas Fischer, "Maccabees, Books of," in *ABD* 4: 440b).

267. Cf. von Rad, *Holy War in Ancient Israel*, 1–33.

268. Discussed in Lind, *Ezekiel,* 214, 256-258.

269. Andersen and Freedman, *Amos*, 323.

270. Although Isaiah seldom if ever unites the vocabularies "covenant" and "law," the law which underlies his oracles in Isaiah 1-5 and Isaiah 6-39 is certainly relational. Both Hosea and Isaiah promote much the same critique against violent power, although Hosea's political ethic is based on a Northern Mosaic theology while that of Isaiah is based on a Southern Zion-Davidic theology!

271. Cf. Alex Haley, *Roots* (Garden City, N.J.: Doubleday Company, Inc. 1976).

272. For background information on Isaiah 1-39, see *ABD* 3: 472-490; on Isaiah 40-55, *ABD* 3: 490-501; on Isaiah 56-66, *ABD* 3: 501-506.

273. This neat distribution is again under attack; some are inclined to locate all of 40–66 in Jerusalem.

274. See Ollenburger, *Zion, the City of the Great King,* 150-155.

275. Ollenburger, *Zion, City of the Great King,* 156.

276. This oracle, its source and its relation to eighth century Isaiah and Micah 4:1-4 is discussed in Hans Wildberger, *Isaiah 1–12,* trans. Thomas H. Trapp, (Minneapolis: Fortress Press, 1991), 85-87. He holds that its origin is Isaiah.

277. In Mesopotamia, this cosmic mountain is identified with the temple and even with divinity:

Temple, great "Mast" of the land of Sumer, grown together with heaven and earth,

....

which juts up out of all lands:
the temple is a great mountain; it reaches to the heavens

—cf. Adam Falkenstein und H. von Soden, *Sumerische und akkadische Hymnen und Gebete,* (Zurich/ Stuttgart: Artemis-Verlag, 1953), p. 166 (my trans. from German).

278. Cf. Andersen and Freedman, *Hosea,* 1980, 408; also, cf. 1 Kings 21:24.

279. Cf. my exposition of this segment in Craig C. Broyles and Craig A. Evans, *Writing and Reading the Scroll of Isaiah,* (Leiden, et. al, Brill, 1997), 329-337.

280. Cf. *BDB A Hebrew and English Lexicon of the Old Testament,* (Boston/New York: Houghton Mifflin Company, 1907), 21, on *light* (*'or*) as instruction.

281. Broyles and Evans, *Writing and Reading,* 337.

282. John N. Oswalt, *The Book of Isaiah, chapters 40–46* (Grand Rapids: Eerdmans, 1998), 3–19.

283. Cf. Lind, *Monotheism,* 163. The concept of the four *Servant Songs* as a biographical unity secondarily inserted into their present places in the Isaiah text was first presented by Klaus Baltzer, "Zur Formgeschichtlichen Bestimmung der Texte vom Gottes-Knecht im Deutero-Jesaja-Buch, *Probleme biblischer Theologie: Festschrift für Gerhard von Rad zum 70. Geburtstag* (Munich: Kaiser, 1971), 27-43. Tyggve N. D. Mettinger regards Baltzer's biographical literary Gattung as possible but "by no means probable." Furthermore he rejects Bernhard Duhm's theory of four Servant Songs as a special group, and sees the songs as fully integrated into the larger text—cf. Mettinger, *A Farewell to the Servant Songs, A Critical Examination of an Exegetical Axiom* (Lund: C. W. K. Gleerup, 1983), 16-17; 18-28; 44-45. I am skeptical about the four songs as a biographical *Gattung,* but regard them as a somewhat continuous biographical description of a servant's ministry that is presently integrated into the larger text. My special interest is their comparison with the loosely parallel Cyrus poems, especially in regard to violent power, covenant law and justice; this interest I hold to involve the entire text, an examination which I must defer to another day.

284. This principle is found in a progressive law of the book of Deuteronomy: "Only for their own crimes may persons be put to death." For a discussion of this unusual law, cf. Moshe Greenberg, 339. But this radical law does not except the penitent sinner from death, as does Ezekiel.

285. For a discussion of the "name" and its relationship to "love" in the book of Ezekiel, see Lind, *Ezekiel,* 173-175; 290-291.

286. *ABD 1*: 279b

287. "Taken as a whole, the book of Daniel is an apocalypse, under-stood 'as a genre of revelatory literature with a narrative framework, in which a revelation is mediated by an other-worldly being to a human recipient, disclosing a transcendent reality, which is both temporal, in-sofar as it envisages eschatological salvation, and spatial insofar as it involves another supernatural world'"—John J. Collins in *ABD 2*: 31, quoting from Collins, *The Apocalyptic Imagination* (Grand Rapids : William B. Eerdmans, 1998), 4.

288. *ABD 1*: 279.

289. *ANET*: 166.

290. John Collins identifies the Son of Man with the Archangel Michel—*ABD II*, 35.

291. *ABD*, 137-138.

292. For the historic relationship of canonical apocalyptic literature to prophetic literature rather than to wisdom literature, as von Rad sees it, refer to P. D. Hanson, *The Dawn of Apocalyptic* (Philadelphia: Fortress Press, 1975).

293. Clarence Bauman, *The Sermon on the Mount*, 273.

294. Ulrich Luz, *Matthew 1–7, A Continental Commentary*, trans. Wil-helm C. Linss (Minneapolis: Fortress Press, 1980), 44. I am deeply in-debted to Luz throughout this chapter for my understanding of the Sermon.

295. Luz, *Matthew 1–7*, 215.

296. For the *imitation of Jesus* comparable to the idea of the *imitation of Yahweh* in the Old Testament, his suffering of abuse in crucifixion for our redemption, see 1 Pet. 2:21-25.

297. The Sermon on the Mount is the good news of blessing, a new way of life, of community. In his teachings and healings, in his subse-quent death and resurrection, Jesus connects this community with the rule of heaven. See Luz, *Matthew 1–7*, 208.

298. Bauman, *The Sermon on the Mount*, 111-127.

299. Cf. John Bright, *Jeremiah*, Anchor Bible (Garden City, N.J.: Dou-bleday & Company, Inc., 1959), 169

300. Luz, *Matthew 1–7*, 280

301. Ibid. I am indebted to Luz's analysis for this, my simplified structure of the Sermon.

302. Luz, *Matthew 1–7*, 213.

303. Luz, *Matthew 1–7*, 375-377, contra Hans Dieter Betz, 374-375.

304. Richard B. Gardner, *Matthew*, Believers Church Bible Commen-tary (Scottdale, Pa.: Herald Press, 1991), 118.

305. Gardner, *Matthew*, 119

306. The Greek original of the Lord's Prayer uses the passive form of the verb ("may your name *be made holy*," emphasis added) found ear-lier in the Old Testament Greek translation of Ezek. 36:23.

307. See my statement, "A Moral Interpretation of History" in *Ezekiel*, 319-321.

308. Gardner, *Matthew*, 119.

309. Cf. Bauman, *The Sermon on the Mount*, 111-127.

310. Cf. Luz, *Matthew 1–7*, 380.

311. Cf. William F. Arndt, and Wilbur F. Gingrich, *A Greek-English Lexicon of the New Testament* (Chicago: The University of Chicago Press; Cambridge: University Press, 1957), 603.

312. Forgiveness of money debt was practiced in ancient Babylon in the eighteenth-seventeenth centuries B.C., by edict at the beginning of a king's reign and every seventh year thereafter (*ANET*, 1968, 526).

313. 2 Cor. 8:8-15. See "*The Justice of God in Paul and Jesus*," in Marshall, *Beyond Retribution*, 38-93

314. *The Goshen News* (December 20, 2001: A-3. Used by permission.

315. See Arndt and Gingrich, 342. On the Jews and Lex Talionis see Marshall, *Beyond Retribution*: 78-84.

316. See Willard M. Swartley, "Matthew: Emmanuel, Power for Peacemaking," chapter three in his forthcoming book. [tentative title: "The Missing Peace in New Testatment Theology and Ethics]

317. Eighteenth century B.C., *ANET*, 1969: 175

318. For an extended discussion of Romans 13:1-7 with reference to New Testament literature, see Marshall, *Beyond Retribution*, 234–239.

319. Jonathan Clarke. "The Conceptual Poverty of U.S. Foreign Policy." *Atlantic Monthly* 272, no. 3 (Mar. 1993), 63.

320. I realize that the *alien* of Nineveh is not quite the equivalent of the *resident alien* within Israel. But may there have been some relationship in the development of love for the *resident alien* (Lev. 19:34) to the extension of the principle stated in Exod. 34:6 to the foreigner in Jonah 4:2? Perhaps the answer to this question is not to be discovered by a purely linguistic approach?

321. Tom Yoder Neufeld, "Power, Love, and Creation, the Mercy of the Divine Warrior in the Wisdom of Solomon" in *Peace and Justice shall Embrace*, ed. Grimsrud and Johns, 174-191. This perceptive article makes a significant contribution to the understanding of *imitatio Dei*.

322. Willard M. Swartley discusses Jesus' teaching about love to one's enemies and Jesus' seemingly unloving conduct against his Pharisee enemies, graphically portrayed in Matthew 23. He asks the question which the reader may want to discuss: "Does love of enemy and 'nonresistance' or non-retaliation ever express itself through words of judgment?"—Swartley, "Matthew: Emmanuel, Power for Peacemaking" (work in progress).

323. Hans Dieter Betz, *The Sermon on the Mount*, 97a.

324. *New York Times Book Review* (December 10, 2000), 34.

325. Sarat, *When the State Kills*.

326. Sarat, *When the State Kills*, from the back cover jacket.

327. Sarat, *When the State Kills*, 13-14.

328. Sarat, *When the State Kills*, vii-viii.

329. Robert Cover, "The Supreme Court, 1982 Term-Foreward: Nomos and Narrative," in *Harvard Law Review* 97 (1983): 34, 39.

330. Sarat, *When the State Kills*, 182.

331. Stephen L. Carter, *The Culture of Disbelief. How American Law and Politics Trivialize Religious Devotion* (New York: Basic Books, 1993), 105.

332. Ibid.

333. These conversations took place over a number of years while they were colleagues teaching their respective specialties at the University of Notre Dame.

334. Thomas L. Shaffer, *Moral Memoranda from John Howard Yoder, Conversations on Law, Ethics, and the Church between a Mennonite Theologian and a Hoosier Lawyer* (Eugene, Ore.: Wipf and Stock Publishers, 2002), iii.

335. Shaffer, *Moral Memoranda*, 114.

336. The Schleitheim Confession, 1527.

337. Shaffer, *Moral Memoranda*, iii.

338. Shaffer, *Moral Memoranda*, iii.

339. Howard John Loewen, "The Schleitheim Confession, 1527," *One Lord, One Church, One Hope, and One God: Mennonite Confessions of Faith in North America: An Introduction* (Elkhart, Ind.: Institute of Mennonite Studies,1985), 80.

340. Shaffer, *Moral Memoranda*, iii.

341. Shaffer, *Moral Memoranda*, iv.

342. Shaffer, *Moral Memoranda*, vi.

343. Shaffer, *Moral Memoranda*, vi.

BIBLIOGRAPHY

ABD 1-VI: *Anchor Bible Dictionary*. Freedman, David Noel, ed. New York et. al.: Doubleday, 1992.

ANET: Ancient Near Eastern Texts. Pritchard, James B., ed. Princeton: Princeton University Press, 1969, third ed.

Andersen, Francis I. and Freedman, David Noel. *Hosea: A New Translation with Introduction and Commentary*. Anchor Bible. Garden City, N. J.: Doubleday & Company, Inc., 1980.

————. *Amos*. Anchor Bible. New York, et. al.: Doubleday, 1989.

Arndt, William F. and Gingrich, F. Wilbur. *A Greek-English Lexicon of the New Testament*. Chicago: The University of Chicago Press; Cambridge: University Press, 1957.

BDB: Brown, Francis and Driver, S. R. and Briggs, Charles A. *A Hebrew and English Lexicon of the Old Testament*. Boston/New York: Houghton Mifflin Company, 1907.

Bauman, Clarence. *The Sermon on the Mount: The Modern Quest for its Meaning*. Macon, Ga.: Mercer University Press, 1985.

Berman, Harold J. *Law and Revolution: The Formation of the Western Legal Tradition*. Cambridge: Harvard University Press, 1983.

Betz, Hans Dieter. *The Sermon on the Mount,* Hermeneia. Philadelphia: Fortress Press, 1995.

Beyerlin, Walter. "Die Paranese in Bundesbuch und ihr Herkunft," 9-29, in *Gottes Wort und Gottes Land,* ed. Henning Graf Reventlow. Göttingen: Vandenhoeck & Ruprecht, 1965.

179

Boecker, Hans Jochen. *Law and the Administration of Justice in the Old Testament and Ancient East*. Trans. Jerry Moiser. Minneapolis: Augsburg Publishing House, 1980.

Boling, Robert G. *Joshua*. Anchor Bible. Garden City / New York: Doubleday & Company, Inc., 1982.

Bonner, Leah. *The Stories of Elijah and Elisha as Polemics Against Baal Worship*. Leiden: E. J. Brill, 1968.

Brenneman, James E. "Prophets in Conflict: Negotiating Truth in Scripture" in *Peace and Justice Shall Embrace, Power and Theopolitics in the Bible: Essays in Honor of Millard Lind*. Ed. Ted Grimsrud and Loren L. Johns. Telford, Pa.: Pandora Press U.S., 1999.

Bright, John. *Jeremiah*. Anchor Bible. Garden City, N.J.: Doubleday & Company, Inc., 1959.

Brown, Raymond E. *The Gospel According to John (i-xii)*. Garden City, N.J.: Doubleday & Company, Inc., 1966.

Broyles, Craig C. and Craig A. Evans. *Writing and Reading the Scroll of Isaiah*. Leiden, et. al.: Brill, 1997.

Brueggemann, Walter. *Genesis, A Bible Commentary for Teaching and Preaching*. Atlanta: John Knox Press, 1982.

Buttrick, Arthur George, ed., *The Interpreters Dictionary of the Bible III*. New York, Nashville: Abingdon Press, 1962.

Campbell, Antony F.. *Of Prophets and Kings, a Late Ninth-Century Document (1 Sam. 1-2 Kings 10)*. Washington, D.C.: The Catholic Biblical Association of America, 1986.

Carter, Stephen L.. *The Culture of Disbelief: How American Law and Politics Trivialize Religious Devotion*. New York: Basic Books, 1993.

Childs, Brevard S. *The Book of Exodus*. Old Testament Library. Philadelphia: Westminster Press, 1974.

Clarke, Jonathan. "The Conceptual Poverty of U.S. Foreign Policy." *Atlantic Monthly* 272, no. 3 (March 1993).

Cogan, Mordechai and Tadmor, Hayim. *II Kings, A New Translation with Introduction and Commentary*. Garden City, N.J.: Doubleday & Company, Inc., 1988.

Collins, John J. *The Apocalyptic Imagination: An Introduction To Jewish Apocalyptic Literature*. Grand Rapids: William B. Eerdmans, 1998.

Cover, Robert. "The Supreme Court, 1982 Term-Foreward: Nomos and Narrative." *Harvard Law Review* 97 (1983):34, 39.

Craig, Hardin. *Shakespeare*. Chicago: Scott, Foresman and Company, 1931.

Cross, Frank Moore. *Canaanite Myth and Hebrew Epic: Essays In The History Of The Religion Of Israel* Cambridge, Mass.: Harvard University Press, 1973.

Daube, David. *Studies in Biblical Law*. Cambridge: Cambridge University Press, 1947.

Dietrich, Walter. *David, Saul, und die Propheten: Das Verhältnis von Religion und Politik nach des Prophetischen Überlieferungen vom Frühesten Köningtum in Israel*. Stuttgart: W. Kohlhammer, 1987.

Driver G. R and Miles, John C. *The Babylonian Laws*, vol. 1, Legal Commentary. Oxford: at the Clarendon Press, corrected sheets of lst ed., 1956, 1960.

Dunn, James D. G. *Jesus, Paul, and the Law: Studies in Mark and Galatians*. Louisville: Westminster/John Knox Press, 1990.

Durham, John I. *Exodus*. Waco, Tex: Word Books, 1987.

Falkenstein, Adam. und von Soden, H. *Sumerische und Akkadische Hymnen und Gebete*. Zurich/Stuttgart: Artemis-Verlag, 1953.

Fohrer, Georg. *Elia. AThANT*. Zurich: Zwingli Verlag, 1957.

Freedman, David Noel. "Pentateuch." *The Interpreters Dictionary of the Bible*, vol. 3. Ed. George Arthur Buttrick. Nashville: Abingdon Press, 1962.

———. Editor in Chief. *The Anchor Bible Dictionary*. New York, et. al.: Doubleday, 1992.

———. "Prolegomena." in George Buchanan Gray. *The Forms of Hebrew Poetry: Considered with Special Reference to the Criticism and Interpretation of the Old Testament*. New York: KTAV Publishing House, 1972.

Gardner, Richard B. *Matthew*. Believers Church Bible Commentary. Scottdale, Pa.: Herald Press, 1991.

The Goshen News. December 20, 2001: A-3.

Gray, George Buchanan, *The Forms of Hebrew Poetry*. New York: KTAV Publishing House, 1972.

Gray, John. *I and II Kings; A Commentary*, Philadelphia: Westminster Press, 1975.

Greenberg, Moshe. *Ezekiel 1-20. ABD 2*. Garden City/New York: Doubleday & Company, 1983.

Grimsrud, Ted and Johns, Loren L. *Peace and Justice Shall Embrace Power and Theopolitics in the Bible*. Telford, Pa.: Pandora Press, U.S., 1999.

Guenther, Allen R. *Hosea, Amos*. Believers Church Bible Commentary. Scottdale, Pa.: Herald Press, 1998.

Haley, Alex. *Roots*. Garden City, N. J.: Doubleday & Company, Inc. 1976.

Hanks, Gardner C. *Against the Death Penalty: Christian and Secular Arguments Against Capital Punishment*. Scottdale, Pa.: Herald Press, 1997).

———. *Capital Punishment and the Bible*. Scottdale, Pa.: Herald Press, 2002.

Hanson, Paul D. *The Dawn of Apocalyptic*. Philadelphia Fortress Press, 1975.

_____. "The Theological Significance of Contradiction within the Book of the Covenant." In *Canon and Authority: Essays In Old Testament Religion and Theology*. Ed. George W. Coats and Burke O. Long; with contributions by Peter R. Ackroyd . . . [et al.]. Festschrift für Zimmerli. Philadelphia: Fortress Press, 1977.

Hasse, Richard. *Einführung in das Stadium Keilschriftlicher Rechtsquellen*. Wiesbaden: Otto Harrassowitz, 1965.

Hauser, Alan J. and Russell Gregory. *From Carmel to Horeb; Elijah in Crisis*. Sheffield: The Almond Press, 1990.

Hiebert, Theodore. "Theophany in the Old Testament." *ABD 6:* 505-511.

Holloway, Stephan W. "Kings, Books of." *ABD 4:* 69-83.

Janzen, Waldemar. *Exodus*. Believers Church Bible Commentary. Scottdale: Herald Press, 2000.

Jeremias, Jorg. *Hosea und Amos; Studien zu den Anfängen des Dodekapropheton.*, Tübingen: J. C. B. Mohr Paul Sieback, 1996.

_____. *Theophanie. Die Geschichte einer alttestamentlichen Gattung*. Neukirchen: Verlag des Erziehungsvereins, 1965.

Kaiser, Otto. *Der Prophet Isaiah, Kapitel 13-39*. Göttingen: Vandenhoeck & Ruprecht, 1973.

Kraus, Hans-Joachim. *Prophetie und Politik* in *Theologische Existenz Heute*. München: Chr. Kaiser Verlag, 1952.

Kreider, Alan. "Military Service in the Church Orders," *Journal of Religious Ethics* 31.3 (2003) 414-442.

Lane, Marietta Jaeger. "The Power of Forgiveness." in *The Voice, Murder Victims' Families for Reconciliation*, No. 12 (Fall/Winter, 2000), 4.

Lategan, Bernard C. "Hermeneutics." *ABD 3:* 149-154.

Leicht, Robert. "2000 Jahre in Widerspruch." *Die Zeit*, Marz 31-May 20 (1999).

Lind, Millard C. *Monotheism, Power, Justice, Collected Old Testament Essays*. Elkhart, Ind.: Institute of Mennonite Studies, 1990.

_____. *Ezekiel*. Believers Church Bible Commentary. Scottdale, Pa. Herald Press, 1996.

_____. *Yahweh is a Warrior: The Theology of Warfare in Ancient Israel*. Scottdale, Pa.: Herald Press, 1980.

Loewen, Howard John. *One Lord, One Hope, and One God: Mennonite Confessions of Faith in North America*. Text-Reader Series No. 2. Elkhart, Ind.: Institute of Mennonite Studies, 1985.

Luckenbill, Daniel David. *The Annals of Sennacherib*. Chicago: The University of Chicago Press, 1921.

Lundbom, Jack R. *Jeremiah, A Study in Ancient Hebrew Rhetoric*. Missoula: Society of Biblical Literature, dist. Scholars Press, 1975

Luz, Ulrich. *Matthew 1–7: A Continental Commentary*. Trans. Wilhelm C. Linss. Minneapolis: Fortress Press, 1980.

Lyons, John. *Introduction to Theoretical Linguistics*. Cambridge: Cambridge University Press, 1968.

Marshall, Christopher D. *Crowned with Glory and Honor; Human Rights in the Biblical Tradition*. Telford, Pa.: Pandora Press U.S.

_____. *Beyond Retribution: A New Testament Vision for Justice, Crime and Punishment*. Grand Rapids: Eerdmans, 2001.

Martens, Elmer A. *Old Testament Theology*. Grand Rapids: Baker Book House, 1997

_____. *God's Design: A Focus on Old Testament Theology*. Grand Rapids: Baker Book House, 1981.

———. *Jeremiah*. Believers Church Bible Commentary. Scottdale, Pa.: Herald Press, 1986.

———. *God's Design: A Theology of the Old Testament*. Grand Rapids: Baker Book House, 1994.

Megivern, James J. *The Death Penalty: An Historical and Theological Survey*. New York: Paulist Press, 1997.

Mendenhall, George E. "The 'Vengeance' of Yahweh," in *The Tenth Generation*. Baltimore: The Johns Hopkins University Press, 1973.

_____. "Covenant Forms in Israelite Tradition." *Biblical Archeologist* 17 (1954): 50-76.

The Mennonite Encyclopedia, vol. 3, ed. Harold S. Bender, C. Henry Smith. Scottdale, Pa.: Mennonite Publishing House, et al., 1957: 473b; and vol. 5, ed. Cornelius J. Dyck and Dennis D. Martin. Scottdale, Pa.: Mennonite Publishing House, 1990: 511-12.

Mettinger, Tryggve N. D. *A Farewell to the Servant Songs; A Critical Examination Of An Exegetical Axiom*. Lund: C. W. K. Gleerup, 1983.

Nielsen, Eduard, *The Ten Commandments in New Perspective; A Traditio-Historical Approach*. Trans. D. J. Bourke. Naperville, Ind.: A. R. Allenson, 1968.

Neufeld, Tom Yoder. "Power, Love, and Creation, the Mercy of the Divine Warrior in the Wisdom of Solomon." In *Peace and Justice shall Embrace*, ed. Ted Grimsrud and Loren L. Johns. Telford, Pa.: Pandora Press U.S.

New York Times Book Review (December 10, 2000).

Noth, Martin. *Überlieferungsgeschichtliche Studien*,1943. Eng. trans., *The Deuteronomistic History, Journal for the Study of the Old Testament*, Sup. 15. Sheffield, England: Sheffield Academic Press, 1967.

_____. *The History of Israel*. New York: Harper and Brothers, 1958.

Ollenburger, Ben. "Gerhard von Rad's Theory of Holy War." In Gerhard von Rad, *Holy War in Ancient Israel*. Trans. Marva J. Dawn. Grand Rapids: Eerdmans, 1991.

_____. Zion, City of the Great King: A Theological Symbol of the Jerusalem Cult. Sheffield: JSOT Press, 1987.

Oswalt, John N. The Book of Isaiah, Chapters 40–46. Grand Rapids: Eerdmans, 1998.

Otto, Susanne. Jehu, Elia und Elisa; Die Erzählung von der Jehu-Revolution und die Komposition der Elia-Elisa-Erzählungen. Stuttgart: Verlag W. Kohlhammer, 2002.

Patrick, Dale. Old Testament Law. Atlanta: John Knox Press, 1985.

Paul, Shalom M. Studies in the Book of the Covenant in the Light of Cuneiform and Biblical Law. Leiden: E. J. Brill, 1970.

Perry, John. "Not Pledging as Liturgy: Lessons from Karl Barth and American Mennonites on Refusing National Oaths." Mennonite Quarterly Review 84 (Oct. 2002): 431-59.

Rad, Gerhard von. "Justice, Human and Divine in the Old Testament." WCC Study Department, Study Conference at Treysa, Germany, Aug. 2-7, 1950 in The Biblical Doctrine of Justice.

_____. The Message of the Prophets. New York: Harper & Row, 1967.

_____. Studies in Deuteronomy. Trans. David Stalker. Chicago: Henry Regnery Company, 1953.

_____. Holy War in Ancient Israel. Trans. Marva J. Dawn. Grand Rapids: Eerdmans, 1991.

Richardson, M. E. J. Hammurabi's Laws: Text, Translation and Glossary. Sheffield: Sheffield Academic Press, 2000.

Robbins, David L. The End of the War, A Novel of the Race for Berlin. New York: Bantam Book, 2000.

Roop, Eugene F. Genesis. Believers Church Bible Commentary. Scottdale, Pa.: Herald Press, 1987

Sarat, Austin. When the State Kills: Capital Punishment and the American Condition. Princeton, N.J.: Princeton University Press, 2001.

The Schleitheim Confession,1527 B.C. See Loewen, Howard John. One Lord, One Hope, and One God, Mennonite Confessions of Faith in North America. Text-Reader Series No. 2, Elkhart, Ind.: Institute of Mennonite Studies, 1985, 79-82.

Schrader, Eberhard, Heinrich Zimmern, and Hugo Winckler. Die Keilsinschriften un das Alte Testament. Berlin: Reuther & Reichard, 1902.

Seow, C. L. "Hosts, Lord of." in ABD 3: 305a.

Shaffer, Thomas L. Moral Memoranda from John Howard Yoder: Conversations on Law, Ethics, and the Church Between a Mennonite Theologian and a Hoosier Lawyer. Eugene, Ore.: Wipf and Stock Publishers, 2002.

Simons, Menno. *The Complete Writings of Menno Simons, C. 1496-1561.* Trans. from the Dutch by Leonard Verduin. Ed. John Christian Wenger. Scottdale, Pa.: Herald Press, 1956.

Sonsino, Rifat. *Motive Clauses in Hebrew Law, biblical forms and Near Eastern Parallels.* Chico: Scholars Press, 1980.

Steck, Odil Hannes. *Überlieferung und Zeitgeschichte in den Elia-Erzählungen.* Neukirchen-Vluyn: Verlag des Erziehungsvereins, 1968.

Swartley, Willard M., ed. *Essays on Biblical Interpretation, Anabaptist-Mennonite Perspectives.* Elkhart, Ind.: Institute of Mennonite Studies, 1984.

_____. *Slavery, Sabbath, War, and Women.* Scottdale, Pa.: Herald Press, 1983.

Utzschneider, Helmut. *Gottes länger Atem: die Exoduserzählung (Ex 1-14) in ästhetischer und historischer Sicht.*

Stuttgart : Verlag Katholisches Bibelwerk,1996.

Weinfeld, Moshe. "Deuteronomy, Book of,"in *ABD* 2: 168-183.

Westermann, Claus. *Genesis 1–11, A Commentary.* Trans. John J. Scullion. Minneapolis: Augsburg, 1984.

White, Marsha C. *The Elijah Legends and Jehu's Coup.* Atlanta: Scholars Press, 1997

Wildberger, Hans. *Isaiah 1–12.* Trans. Thomas H. Trapp. Minneapolis: Fortress Press, 1991.

Winkler, H. See Schrader above.

Wolff, Hans Walter. *Hosea, A Commentary on the Book of the Prophet Hosea.* Trans. Gary Stansell Philadelphia: Fortress Press, 1974.

_____"The Kerygma of the Deuteronomic Historical Work." In *The Vitality of Old Testament Traditions.* Ed. Walter Brueggemann and Hans Walter Wolff. Atlanta: John Knox Press, 1976.

Würthwein, Ernst. "Elijah at Horeb: 'Reflections on 1 Kings 19:9-18'." In *Studien zur Deuteronomistischen Geschichtswerk.* Berlin: Walter de Gruyter, 1994.

The Author

Raised on several farms near Albany, Oregon after his 1918 birth in Bakersfield, California, Millard Lind studied at Hesston (Kan.) College before receiving a B.A. from Goshen (Ind.) College in 1942. After he earned his B.D. degree from Goshen College Biblical Seminary, Lind was pastor at Hopewell Mennonite Church, Kouts, Indiana, until 1947. Next he and family moved to Scottdale, Pennsylvania. There Lind began twelve years on the editorial staff of Mennonite Publishing House and received a Th.M. from Pittsburgh-Xenia Theological Seminary while also serving as pastor of the Kingview Mennonite Church.

During 1960-1990, Lind was Professor of Old Testament at Goshen Biblical and Associated Mennonite Biblical Seminaries until 1990. In 1965 Lind received his Th.D. degree in Old Testament from Pittsburgh Theological Seminary. In the 1960s and 1970s he also studied in Israel and Greece with Hebrew Union College; the American Schools of Oriental Research, East Jerusalem; the Ecumenical Institute at Tantur, Jerusalem. He co-led student study groups to the Near East in 1973 and 1975 and in 1982 led an AMBS fall semester of students abroad, situated in the walled city of Jerusalem. Lind was an associate trustee of the American Schools of Oriental Research 1981-1983 and has had a continuing interest in Middle Eastern archaeology, especially as it relates to the Bible.

Lind reports that *The Sound of Sheer Silence and the Killing State* is an attempt, after half a century of study and teaching, to say what he concludes the Bible is centrally about. A practical source of interest for writing the book came from serving with the College Mennonite Church Peace Ministries Center in an inter-faith effort against capital punishment. From the biblical side, an impulse for the effort was born when he was invited by his pastor to lead a congregational seminar on The Sermon on the Mount. With the class, he considered again the New Testament statement of the unity of the Bible, the nature of the relationship between Moses, Elijah, and Jesus; and was confronted once more with the Bible's claim that it presents for the world an alternative law and justice.

Lind's earlier books included *Yahweh Is a Warrior* (Herald Press, 1980); *Monotheism, Power, Justice* (Institute of Mennonite Studies, 1990); and *Ezekiel* in the Believers Church Bible Commentary (Herald Press, 1996). He has published numerous articles in scholarly and church magazines.

Lind and his wife Miriam live in Goshen, Indiana. They have seven grown children, eighteen grandchildren, and four great-grandchildren.